CHARISMA IN POLITICS, RELIGION AND THE MEDIA

Charisma in Politics, Religion and the Media

Private Trauma, Public Ideals

David Aberbach
Associate Professor of Hebrew and Comparative Literature
McGill University, and
Visiting Academic, London School of Economics

NEW YORK UNIVERSITY PRESS
Washington Square, New York

© David Aberbach 1996

First published in the U.S.A. in 1996 by
NEW YORK UNIVERSITY PRESS
Washington Square
New York, N.Y. 10003

Library of Congress Cataloging-in-Publication Data
Aberbach, David, 1954–
Charisma in politics, religion, and the media : private trauma,
public ideals / David Aberbach.
p.   cm.
Includes bibliographical references and index.
ISBN 0–8147–0647–9
1. Charisma (Personality trait)   2. Gifts, Spiritual.
3. Leadership—Psychological aspects.   4. Political leadership.
5. Leadership—Religious aspects.   I. Title.
BF698.35.C45A24   1996
155.2'32—dc20   95–44389
                                                            CIP

Printed in Great Britain

To Mimi, Gabriella, Shulamit and Jessica
with all my love

Contents

Introduction

'With the death of the soul the walking corpse turns into a totally public being.'

Amos Oz, *Black Box* (1988)

The word 'charisma' is the most enduring, abused and controversial legacy of the German sociologist Max Weber (1864–1920). Weber uprooted the word from its theological provenance and applied it to secular phenomena, above all in politics. Charisma is still used in its religious meaning as 'a free gift or favour vouchsafed by God's grace, a talent' (*OED*)* and perhaps best fits the biblical prophet whose power and appeal lie not in his institutional role as in the force of his personality and message. Under Weber's influence, charisma has expanded uncomfortably to include all sorts of exceptional and unexceptional talents in public and private life. The word is now commonly applied to individuals who have for good or bad left their mark on society, particularly through politics or the media: for example, Adolf Hitler, Franklin D. Roosevelt, Charlie Chaplin and Marilyn Monroe. At the same time, its widespread journalistic use to describe countless lesser public figures most of whom are rapidly forgotten – politicians, actors, singers, boxers, baseball players, football and cricket players, even sports commentators and newsreaders – has given charisma a popular dimension with broad meaning.

Charisma is necessarily defined by its usage, and it has a lively variety of meanings, both casual and profound. The former threaten to rob the word of all meaning; the latter are the main subject of this book. Charismatics shine in three main arenas: politics, religion and the media. Although theologians, historians and sociologists have studied many aspects of charisma in their respective fields, comparative studies are rare. This book adopts an eclectic, comparative approach, emphasizing the paradoxical nature of charisma.

Even in its secular forms, charisma retains a religious dimension. Similarly, traditional religious charisma is rarely devoid of political and other significance. For this reason, the exploration of 'secular' charismatics about whom much is known – Hitler or Chaplin, for example – casts light on the

---

* See, for example, Suenens (1978) and Boff (1985). For extensive bibliography on charisma as a theological and secular concept, see Conger and Kanungo (1988).

nature of charisma in its religious forms where little is known. Conversely, the study of religious charismatics often helps to interpret what seem on the surface to be exclusively secular phenomena, such as the role of Robespierre in the French Revolution or that of Garibaldi in the struggle for Italian independence.

As a result, surprising parallels are found in the lives of individuals who otherwise appear to have little in common apart from their charismatic appeal, for example Marilyn Monroe and Krishnamurti. Both had what I regard as the archetypal background for charismatic potential – a broken and disturbed family in childhood. Both yearned to belong to the Public or the Universe as part of their charismatic role. 'I belonged to the Public and to the world,' confessed Marilyn Monroe, 'because I had never belonged to anything or anyone else' (1974, p. 124), while Krishnamurti for his part declared: 'I belong to all people, to all who really love, to all who are suffering' (Lutyens, 1975, p. 233).

Krishnamurti has a unique place in the history of religion as he was not just a lapsed messiah but also, in his old age, allowed a fully documented critical biography to be written (*ibid*). To do so is rare among messiahs. In its self-revelation, Krishnamurti's biography completed his abnegation of the messianic role. His life story exposes the psychology of religious charisma and of messianism. In his deeper motivations, Krishnamurti was not unlike the film goddess. Both craved to belong, though hurt and disillusioned in private life. Both struggled to achieve union with a higher power, with the Public or the Universe.

A dusty German philosophical tract of 1923 is an unlikely place to find profundities on the origins of charisma. Martin Buber's *I and Thou* is a bible of insight. To Buber, human longings for relation with others and with the cosmic have the same origins, in infancy:

> The innateness of the longing for relation is apparent even in the earliest and dimmest stage. Before any particulars can be perceived, dull glances push into the unclear space toward the indefinite; and at times when there is obviously no desire for nourishment, soft projections of the hands reach, aimlessly to all appearances, into the empty air towards the indefinite (1970, p. 77).

Such spiritual yearnings begin with the infant's bond with its mother and its normal drive to explore and create. The baby's seemingly aimless 'charismatic' appeal – what baby is not charismatic? – has an almost mystical quality. If the baby has mastery over its caregivers who satisfy its needs, this appeal will radiate with quiet confidence mainly towards loved ones. If unsatisfied, this appeal may expand promiscuously into an all-consuming and often-distorted search for compensation, or an over-blown drive for the mastery denied to the infant. In adult life, the charismatic may continue to reach 'toward the indefinite', to merge with a greater being; or he may seek unity with society or humanity at large, through the mastery of a medium such as religion, politics, literature, music or film.

Is this reaching out a form of immaturity? Is it self-creation with the aim of richer maturity? Is public recognition and acceptance of the charismatic a betrayal of some societal flaw, or a means of overcoming it? Does the charismatic inevitably create a 'new identity', a semi-mythic persona, out of a character split and distorted by childhood griefs? Or is this persona in fact real, and always latent within? The charismatic, no doubt, incorporates this persona into a wider social or political entity. In this way, the lack of parents, or of secure parental authority, can be turned to advantage. Billy Wilder, director of Marilyn Monroe in *Some Like It Hot*, commented acidly: 'The question really is whether Marilyn is a real person or one of the greatest synthetic products ever invented.' The same question might be asked of charismatics generally. The actress herself spoke of 'Marilyn' as her creation, a product of much calculation, a fabricated superstructure without a foundation. Unlike the orphan girl she had been, 'Marilyn' belonged 'to the ocean and the sky and the whole world' (1974, p. 25). This persona was diametrically opposed to the woman's self-image, which more closely resembled a Francis Bacon painting. Through such personae, the charismatic may struggle to master grief or disability. Charismatic 'appeal' has two meanings: a powerful aesthetic attraction to the public, and a cry for help artfully disguised or transcended. The public response to charisma is not just an aesthetic phenomenon but it is sometimes also a simple human reply to the appeal for help.

The craving for relation, for union with people, objects or abstractions, is at the heart of Buber's philosophy and, in fact, the response which he personally evoked was often that of a charismatic leader. His seeking for charismatic union, described in his book of dialogues, *Daniel* (1913), might be linked with his own horrendous experience of childhood loss:

On a gloomy morning I walked upon the highway, saw a piece of mica lying, picked it up and looked at it for a long time; the day was no longer gloomy, so much light was caught in the stone. And suddenly as I raised my eyes from it, I realized that while I had looked I had not been conscious of 'object' and 'subject'; in my looking that mica and 'I' had been one; in my looking I had tasted unity (1964, p. 140).

According to Buber's biographer, Maurice Friedman (1981), the philosophy of meeting and dialogue sprang out of Buber's experience of severe childhood trauma. When Buber was three, his mother 'disappeared without leaving a trace' (p. 4). He saw her only once afterwards, many years later (p. 11). This loss had an incalculable impact on Buber's life and thought. It was 'the decisive experience of Martin Buber's life, the one without which neither his early seeking for unity nor his later focus on dialogue and on the meeting with the "eternal Thou" is understandable' (p. 15). Such seeking in the aftermath of loss, to compensate for loss, appears to underlie many of the striking cases of charisma.

Charisma in the sense in which I use it in this book grows out of the creative union of emotional (and sometimes physical) disability and unusually developed gifts, perhaps to counterbalance this disability. These gifts come to fruition through an intersection or correspondence between the charismatic's inner world and external social, political and economic reality. The relation between the charismatic and the group is inherently paradoxical. Charisma, Weber noted, exists in relation to a group, especially in crisis. 1789, 1815, 1848, 1861, 1940 are moments of crisis in modern history which have thrust forward charismatic leaders. Yet it can be argued with equal force (e.g. Lasswell, 1960) that these leaders (or some of them) created crisis in a struggle to master and resolve inner disabilities projected on to the public sphere. The motives and needs of the charismatic and the group are often widely disparate and the area of intersection is narrow.

In my view, historical crisis is never entirely new to charismatics such as Robespierre, Lincoln, Roosevelt or Churchill. I mean that they have been schooled in parallel, perhaps harder, crises in their inner lives and are, therefore, well-qualified, as it were, to deal with social, political or military crisis. The craving for resolution might be greater in them than in most individuals. Their motivation is stronger. The role of depression and stimulus is often critical in the emergence of charisma. The charismatic has been crippled to some extent, in spirit or body, and is prone to depression. Consequently, he builds sophisticated means of stimulus for reawakening and strengthening the self. This self-schooling can have social value in time of depression and other social crisis, economic or otherwise. All great charismatics are gifted entertainers. They have the power to uplift and inspire. For them, though, as for their society in crisis, 'entertainment' is no casual pastime. It is a vital means of spiritual and physical survival, an expression of the will to live at a time when destruction or self-destruction may be imminent. Like all forms of energy, charisma is not itself good or bad, neither is it ever a neutral quantity. It can appear in various guises and intensities. Yet it always points the way to change, whether through creation or destruction.

The unusual way in which this book evolved over a period of many years helps to explain my approach to charisma. It grew first out of a study of literature and psychology, and only after that from the traditional fields in studies of charisma – sociology, history and religion. As an Oxford graduate student in 1975–7, I wrote a thesis on the Hebrew poet Chaim Nachman Bialik (1873–1934). This thesis was not specifically about charisma, but it touched on aspects of Bialik's exceptional, perhaps unique, charismatic appeal. Bialik spoke with the violent passionate force of the biblical prophets, Weber's models for the charismatic type. His impact upon the Jewish people and the Zionist movement was probably comparable in its time to that of Isaiah or Jeremiah in theirs. The concept of charisma was helpful in making sense of the dynamic bond between Bialik's inner world as revealed in his poetry and external social and political reality which he addressed in his public role. I explored this correlation in articles for *Encounter, Midstream, Moznayim, Hebrew Union College Annual* and *Prooftexts*, culminating in a book-length study of Bialik (1988).

My interest in creative writers such as Bialik led me to work with children, many from broken homes, while training in child psychotherapy at the Tavistock Clinic (1980–2). Practical experience influenced my thinking on the role of childhood loss in creativity, including mysticism and charisma. These ideas were fleshed out in a series of articles for *The International Review of Psycho-Analysis* and in my book *Surviving Trauma: loss, literature and psychoanalysis* (1989). This book, interestingly, aroused strong animosity among literary critics and equally strong acceptance among those who work with people. Having studied the inner world of the charismatic, or what is known of it, I became increasingly interested in charisma as an historical and sociological phenomenon. In the latter stage of this book, I spent two stimulating years (1992–3, 1994–5) as Academic Visitor in the Department of Sociology, London School of Economics. This book, then, represents an attempt to bridge two disciplines – psychology and the social sciences – and two very different approaches to human nature. It attempts, perhaps not very successfully, to synthesize two conflicting perceptions of where truth lies: in government and the exercise of power, and the holiness and unholiness of the heart's affections.

Still, the starting point of this book was not a religious or political leader, but a poet. Bialik shared with many other writers the experience of childhood loss. He writes of the death of his father when he was six and his separation from his mother soon after as the pivotal crisis of his life, motivating his creativity and his public role. As an orphan, Bialik could best speak for his 'orphaned', uprooted people. He could express their sense of victimization and ruin, their sorrow, anger and frustration, and their longing to be reunited with an idealized ancestral motherland. Bialik is unusual as the correspondence between his public role and his inner life is clear. I began to ask myself if a similar correspondence exists in other charismatic leaders. This book argues that it does.

The chapters on Hitler, Chaplin and Bialik appeared in slightly different form in *Encounter*, and some of the material on Krishnamurti, Marilyn Monroe and John Lennon was first published, also in a changed form, in *Surviving Trauma* and in *Harvard Theological Review*. The ideas on charisma and attachment theory in this book are elaborated upon in a recently-published article of mine in the *International Journal of Psycho-Analysis*.

Throughout this time, I have been blessed with a most loving, patient and interested wife, and to Mimi and our darling daughters, Gabriella, Shulamit and Jessica, this book is dedicated.

1 Political Charisma: Crisis and Paradox

'Where danger is, the saving also flourishes.'
Hölderlin

Many historical crises of the past two hundred years are inseparable from individual leaders whom historians and sociologists (e.g. Weber, 1968; Schlesinger, 1960; Shils, 1965; Schweitzer, 1974; Willner, 1984) often describe as charismatic or having charismatic qualities. Did crisis create them or did they create crisis? If so, why? Were they indispensable in achieving social change, or were they tools in the hands of those whom they led, or of blind forces over which they had little or no control? These perennial red herrings are the quintessential paradoxes which, in my view, define charisma. Charisma is the question mark that forms scabbily with the clash of the inner world of the individual in power with social and political crisis.

While the nature of charisma precludes the existence of a standard, predictable charismatic personality, the greatest political charismatics are not unlike artists. They use their followers as 'material' to raise politics to the level of art. They draw on subconscious motives and drives, using the full force of their imagination to extend the possibilities of existence, for good or evil. The Promethean daring of the charismatic links him with the great artists who expand our sense of what we are and of life's rich possibilities. Ann Ruth Willner (1984) writes in *The Spellbinders: Charismatic Political Leadership*: 'The charismatic leader is in a sense the Prometheus of politics who also steals from the gods by stretching political reality beyond the bounds of belief and prediction' (p. 201).

Can the impact of such leaders be gauged? One familiar approach is to try to imagine the course of history had a charismatic leader died prior to the crisis which brought him to power: if, for example, Robespierre had been executed in 1789 instead of 1794; if Lincoln had been assassinated in 1861, not 1865; if Garibaldi had been shot dead in one of his many battles and skirmishes as a renegade in South America in the 1830s and 1840s; if Herzl's heart condition had killed him in 1897, the year he founded the World Zionist Organization, rather than 1904; if Fanny Kaplan's assassination attempt on Lenin in 1918 or Joseph Zangara's attempt on

1

Franklin D. Roosevelt's life in 1933 had succeeded; if Churchill's car accident in New York in 1931 had been fatal; if Hitler's generals had murdered him in 1940. Such speculation costs and changes nothing, but it forces us to confront the paradox that modern democratic society has been shaped to an unconscionable and totally unpredictable degree by a handful of individuals.

At the same time, in a further paradox, charismatic leaders prior to and sometimes even after the crises which raise them to power are often described as ineffectual, banal or unimpressive. J.M. Roberts' shrewd assessment that if not for the French Revolution, Robespierre would be 'remembered at best as an ornament of the Arras bar' (1978, p. 93) might be generally true of the relationship between crisis and charisma. To many observers during the Revolution, Robespierre seemed no more than a little clerk or a tailor of the *ancien régime*, 'a pure nonentity', as Simon Schama puts it (1989, p. 577). Biographers are regularly struck dumb by the transformation of seemingly ordinary, even mediocre men into charismatic leaders. Douglas Freeman (1948–57), for example, cannot explain George Washington: 'The transformation . . . of the quiet Virginia planter into the revered continental commander [is] beyond documentary explanation' (III, xiii). Though Washington in his lifetime became a cult figure in the United States, he had no outstanding talent, no burning wish to bring about radical change, no distinction in gaining power and using it (Schwartz, 1987).

Even indisputably crucial leaders, such as Garibaldi, Lincoln and Lenin, who live in history in a semi-mythical glow, are characterized by their apparent ordinariness, their disappointing lack of charismatic appeal prior to the crises which lifted them to power. This is not just a narrative trick by which the later achievement is made to seem all the more amazing in view of its unpromising start. Garibaldi – short, bow-legged, humourless, hardly seemed remarkable in the early part of his career, when his influence was slight (Hibbert, 1965). Lincoln, with thin neck, high-pitched voice, ill-fitting clothes, did not cut an impressive figure (Brogan, 1935, p. 73). Gandhi, too, according to his biographer Louis Fischer, gave little sign of future greatness:

> The contrast between the mediocre, unimpressive, handicapped, floundering M.K. Gandhi, barrister-at-law, who left England in 1891, and the Mahatma leader of millions is so great as to suggest that until public service tapped his enormous reserves of intuition, will power, energy and self-confidence, his true personality remained dormant (1982, p. 43).

Even Lenin up to 1917 seemed less a charismatic figure than a provincial grocer, writes Clark (1988): 'A most ordinary-looking man' – this is how Stalin remembered Lenin, echoing many others before they, too, came under Lenin's spell – 'below average height, in no way, literally in no way, distinguishable from ordinary mortals' (p. 110). The indifference which Lenin could arouse before Russia became desperate to get out of the world war is illustrated amusingly in an anecdote told by his wife, Krupskaya. In 1916, the summer before the Revolution, Lenin was still unknown. On holiday in the Swiss Alps, the couple met a Russian soldier on leave: 'Vladimir Ilyich hovered about him like a cat after lard, tried several times to engage him in a conversation about the predatory character of the war; the fellow . . . was clearly not interested' (*ibid.*, pp. 176–7).

Within a few months, however, the Russian army was so badly beaten that the defence of the Revolution was preferable to being sent to the front. Only at this point, in April 1917, did Lenin achieve charisma with a critical mass of Russians, when he made his dramatic journey in the sealed train from Zurich to Petrograd.

Even Churchill, as we shall see in Chapter 2, failed to achieve a charismatic bond with the British public until the war; before that, in the 1930s, he *lacked* charisma as his belligerent style was out of step with the times.

The most blatantly underestimated of modern charismatics was Hitler. In the early years of his career in the 1920s, and even after he came to power, Hitler was often dismissed as a ridiculous clown. This impression was strengthened by his Chaplin moustache, his ungrammatical German, hysterical ravings and, until 1930, his lack of broad popular appeal. Ian Kershaw (1991) characterizes Hitler during his first thirty years as a 'nobody': 'Adolf Hitler's early life offered not a single hint of the figure who was to make the world hold its breath. It seemed rather to point to a future of insignificance and mediocrity' (p. 1). Apart from his fanatical conviction which made him extraordinary, Hitler was indeed a mediocrity on a purely personal level. Kershaw makes the general observation that 'the mass appeal of a "charismatic" leader has only an indifferent relation to that leader's actual personality and character attributes. Perceptions are more important than reality' (p. 48).

What, then, sets the charismatic leader apart? Most important is the singleminded conviction of being chosen by Destiny for a great heroic mission. This mission becomes clear in crisis. Napoleon would often speak of his Destiny (Butterfield, 1962, p. 81); Garibaldi believed firmly that Destiny had marked him for triumph, and his fearlessness in battle and power to inspire men came from this unswerving conviction (Hibbert, 1965, p. 364); Lenin's atheism did not stop him believing devoutly that he and he alone was chosen by Destiny to lead the Revolution (Clark, 1988, p. 170); Churchill felt that Destiny had prepared him all through his life for the trial of leading Britain through the war (Gilbert, 1983, VI 317); and de Gaulle was conscious of his Destiny long before 1940 (Mauriac, 1966, p. 13).

In crisis, the charismatic leader rises from the ordinary, to be transformed and fulfil this destined role. Even Napoleon would probably have remained an obscure soldier with a limited command if not for the crisis which brought him to power and galvanized and stretched his intellect. The Duke of Wellington said of Napoleon that his presence on the battlefield was worth forty thousand men – some might call this an understatement – but what if there had been no battlefield? Aspiring charismatics might welcome crisis – even try to create it – in order to emerge from the ordinary, to break out of the cell of themselves and their painfully narrow world, to give scope to their latent gifts, to forge their transcendent role. The attraction of crisis to opportunists of all sorts is made clear by Richard Cobb in his book on the French Revolution (1972):

> Revolutionary periods are, of course, particularly rich in both accident and chance, and thus offer a tempting premium to all those for whom, in the normal course of events, the promise of sudden change, promotion, enrichment, excitement, had seemed definitely excluded. This is another way of saying that a revolutionary crisis, in any of its constantly changing and rapidly developing phases, offers not just one, but a series, of chances to those who had done badly in life or who had been done badly by life, to better themselves (p. 64).

The charismatic leader is prepared to take unusually risky, dramatic chances. In doing so, he transforms routine so completely that when he temporarily stoops to the ordinary – Garibaldi, for example, once applied for a job in the New York Post Office – he seems extraordinary, even ludicrous, in retrospect.

Crisis creates charisma. If not for the French Revolution, Robespierre almost certainly would not have risen to a position of extreme power and influence. Napoleon would not have become Emperor of France. If not for crises in Italy and Germany, Garibaldi and Bismarck would probably not have emerged as great national leaders. If not for the crisis over slavery, Lincoln might not have become president of the United States. If not for the crisis in Russia caused by World War I – the appalling casualties, the bread shortage, the breaking of civilian and military spirit at the same time under the weight of inefficiency and corruption – Lenin would probably have remained unknown to his dying day, a crackpot revolutionary in exile. If not for the Nazi threat in 1940, Churchill would not have come to power; and de Gaulle, similarly, was 'the man of the abyss, irresistibly summoned and virtually created by the void that disaster creates' (Mauriac, p. 37). The 'if not's echo through history.

And yet, does crisis create charisma? Is it not also true that charisma provokes crisis? In this paradox the dynamic nature of charisma lies. If charisma is defined in terms of achievement and change through crisis, the great charismatics had decisive personal power. Much as Robespierre, for example, was created by the Revolution, he also helped to make it and enable it to succeed. He personified its character and direction. Far from being 'a pure nonentity', David Jordan writes, Robespierre became one of the great movers in history:

> Robespierre is one of those rare figures in history who are perceived by their contemporaries as well as posterity as embodying the essence of the passion and contradictions of their historical moment, who seem to personify an age or a movement; whose lives represent general propositions about significant human experience (1985, p. 3).

In other historical crises, too, the charismatic leader was crucial. Abraham Lincoln, in D.W. Brogan's view, decided the outbreak of the American Civil War in 1861: 'it is possible that if the war had not come in 1861, it might never have come at all' (p. 84). Garibaldi, more than any man with the possible exception of Cavour, ensured the unification of Italy in the 1860s (as Bismarck did Germany at the same time). Herzl created an international Zionist organization and set in motion the political process leading to the creation of the State of Israel. Lenin's personal role was indispensable in the Bolshevik revolution. Roosevelt's leadership created the legislation and the spirit which helped lift America from the Depression in the 1930s. Churchill's forceful leadership, especially in 1940–1, helped to ensure the eventual defeat of Nazism. As for Hitler, the role of personal charisma is of the essence, Robert Waite writes:

> The political system he established was dependent ultimately upon the power of his person, the efficacy of his charisma. He *was* Nazism. Since he was the sole source of final authority, he alone could legitimize Party decisions and determine public policy. His personal whim became the law of the land; his will decided war or peace in the world. Seldom in the history of Western civilization since Jesus has so much depended on one man's personality (in Langer, 1972, p. 220).

The charismatic leader, transformed from the ordinary, has a parallel effect on his followers, who are now able and ready to do extraordinary deeds and, if need be, give up their lives. (Of the leaders mentioned so far, Herzl and Gandhi were the only ones who did not send men to their deaths.) Unfortunately, in the long run, this mutual transformation rarely benefits the people led. Charismatics express 'the people's will', but often, in yet another paradox, they steer their followers towards goals which are at best a mixed blessing and at worst a total disaster. The Reign of Terror instituted by Robespierre was hardly in the best interests of France, nor, in the end, were the Napoleonic wars. Bismarck's success in uniting Germany set it on a militant course leading to two world wars; and even Garibaldi's unification of Italy, writes Denis Mack Smith, was not to the advantage of the Italian masses, the poor, the uneducated, or the devout Catholics: 'There can be little doubt that Garibaldi's prestige among ordinary people helped to obscure what was really happening until they were too late to resist it' (1956, p. 68). The same could be said of Lenin who, once in power, instituted a form of government which proved ruinous to Russia. Hitler, who claimed and was believed to have the sure instinct of a sleepwalker, led Germany over the cliff of defeat.

The prospect of failure is rarely envisaged in the first mutual, desperate recognition of leader and followers in crisis. This recognition has the spontaneous force of unrestrained, uncritical love. When Lenin arrived in Petrograd in 1917, he embraced the anarchic conditions which made a charismatic bond possible. In one fatal moment, nation and leader, bonded in crisis, were changed utterly. Lenin went from being largely unknown and nondescript to international fame, from exiled fanatic to adulated leader, from virtual powerlessness to unprecedented power, from the eccentric fringe to the centre, from theory to practice. This meeting of leader and followers illustrates another side of charisma overlooked at times or taken for granted. It is a triumph of the personal force of one man over impersonal, brutal forces of mechanized warfare. It affirms the value of a single human life at a time when life is drastically cheapened by slaughter. (Chaplin's impact during World War I might, similarly, be ascribed in part to the effects of the war.) Ronald Clark describes this moment, when Lenin's fate and that of Russia hung in the balance:

Any fears that Lenin may have had about his reception in Russia vanished as soon as the train steamed into Petrograd's Finland Station. A supporter wrote: 'At last . . . the lighted windows of the carriages began to twinkle – more and more gently and slowly. The train stopped, and at once we perceived, over the crowd of workers, the figure of Comrade Lenin. Lifting Ilyich high above their heads the Sestroretsk workers conducted him into the station hall.' Hindsight at first suggests that the Provisional Government's failure to prevent Lenin from getting his grip on the crowds from the moment of arrival was a grave mistake of tactics; in fact it was no more than an indication that even now the Government's influence was patchy and irresolute compared with that which Lenin's charisma could exercise almost whenever he wished (p. 209).

The paradox of crisis and charisma is illumined in this moment of high drama. Crisis creates the need for heroic leadership. Yet, the charismatic, in turn, may make all the difference in the outcome. Charisma and crisis are dynamic, interlocking forces, feeding on and manipulating each other. It is rarely clear to what extent the leader decides or follows events, gives his followers what they want or creates in them the desires which he satisfies. If not for Lincoln, as we have seen, the American Civil War might not have broken out, yet Lincoln himself admitted in 1864: 'I claim not to have controlled events, but confess plainly that events have controlled me' (1957, p. 265).

The meaning of a charismatic relationship must lie in the interconnection between external crisis and the inner world of the charismatic. As usual, there is a paradox here as well. The charismatic is a public being, an open book, about whom much is known. At the same time, the inner world, the past, the motives, drives and hopes of the charismatic are mostly hidden. What is revealed is often extremely limited and distorted. Charisma involves a virtual state of amnesia toward the past, or suppression of the past. It is the charismatic's gift to make large numbers of people forget the past, forget themselves temporarily, and live vividly in the spell of the present. The fact that the charismatic appears to slough off his past and private life and creates a new, public identity is a serious handicap as well as a source of fascination to biographers. François Mauriac makes this point emphatically about de Gaulle. From the moment de Gaulle assumed leadership of the Free French in 1940, 'the history of de Gaulle is the history made by de Gaulle. He no longer has a private life' (p. 68). However, de Gaulle's private life before 1940 is mostly obscure. A biography of a charismatic leader typically gives a tiny fraction of space to the period until the crisis which brought him to power – e.g. Robespierre (b. 1758) might get thirty pages, or a page a year, until 1789; Lenin (b. 1871), perhaps fifty pages for the forty-six years until 1917 – whereupon the 'real' biography begins. There are exceptions, notably Churchill, but even these teach us relatively little about the childhood, the inner life and the feelings of the charismatic hero. The biography of a great man is rarely, if ever, the revelation of the man as he was. It arises from a fascination with the largely fictional public image which he created and a consequent desire to find the 'real' man and his motives, despite the lack of conclusive documentation.

A case in point is Alan Bullock's biography of Ernest Bevin. Bullock gives a totally absorbing portrait of the trade unionist, minister of labour in Churchill's war cabinet and foreign minister in the Atlee government. Yet in the space of three volumes totalling over two thousand pages, there is virtually no insight into the inner world of a man who in 1909 was a carter delivering mineral water in Bristol and by the 1930s headed the largest trade union in the world – the Transport and General Workers Union – which he had almost singlehandedly brought into being. How did this transformation come about?

What we know of political and religious charismatics usually comes from secondary, not first-hand sources. As suggested earlier, however, there is a pattern of distortion and upheaval in the childhood of many of the great charismatics. Robespierre, for example, was deeply scarred by his mother's death when he was six and his father's subsequent abandonment of the surviving family (Rudé, 1975). Lincoln's mother died when he was nine (Brogan, p. 14). Garibaldi's father was away at sea for much of his childhood (Hibbert, p. 4). Bismarck suffered a painful, if obscure, sense of 'alienation' in his early family life (Gall, 1990, p. 3). The death of Lenin's father and the execution of his brother for plotting to murder the Tsar were crucial factors in turning him into a revolutionary (Clark, pp. 12–20). Paderewski lost his mother a few months after birth (Zamoyski, 1982, p. 7). Stalin lost three siblings in early childhood and his father at eleven (Deutscher, 1989, pp. 22, 24). Hitler and his family suffered multiple losses culminating in the deaths of his father at fourteen and his mother at seventeen (Langer, 1972; Waite, 1977). To these we may add the leader of the most significant twentieth century revolution after 1917, the Ayatollah Khomeini, whose father was killed when he was an infant (Algar, 1985, p. 13).

These are admittedly major traumas for children to bear, and it may be inferred that they were far more important in the development of the inner life of the charismatic than any external social or political reality. Yet, remarkably, in virtually no instance do we have a first-hand account of the immediate and long-range impact of these crises. This silence corroborates the observation made earlier on that charismatic public identity can serve as a tool of amnesia or, like dreams or screen memories, as a means of both expressing the trauma and screening it by transforming it into political motivation.

What remains are usually no more than hints and flashes of speculation such as those of Alan Bullock on the traumatic origins of Bevin's exceptional capacity for leadership:

Despite the affection of his mother, which he remembered with grati-
tude all his life, it had been a hard childhood, with no father, with his
mother dying and his home broken up when he was eight. From his
earliest years he had known need and insecurity; from the age of eleven
he was pushed out into the world to earn his own living. Neither the boy
then nor the man later regarded this as exceptional: it was the common
lot of the labouring class into which he had been born. Forced to look
after himself, he learned to rely on himself; he was laying the foundation of that massive confidence and self-sufficiency which never failed
him (1960 I 6).

What survivals of trauma exist in the charismatic role? There may be
the abstract quest for liberty, unity, union or reunion on a national or
political sphere, the relentless identification with nation or cause. Having
struggled for inner freedom and wholeness, charismatic leaders may be
needed in crisis, when nation, society or government is faced with disunity
and disintegration. (De Gaulle was only half-joking when he remarked
that France could achieve unity only in crisis, for what could one expect
of a country with 265 kinds of cheese!) Self-trained to fight inner discord
and breakdown, charismatics may be best suited in certain conditions to
draw on their personal experience to fight external social breakdown. It is
often pointed out by historians and psychologists as well as sociologists
(e.g. Erikson, 1958; Lasswell, 1960) that a chief attraction of public life
– some would say *the* chief attraction – is that solutions which are nonexistent in the inner world may offer themselves in the public role. Inner
certainty, undesirable and unrealistic in other times, is a source of communal strength in crisis. A rigid ideology, a defence against fragmentation
and uncertainty, gives a society in crisis firm, consistent direction. What
seems to be necessary firmness in crisis might in normal conditions have
a fanatic glare, especially in democratic societies. The charismatic does
not change substantially but functions best in crisis.

De Gaulle is a model of the charismatic leader schooled in crisis whose
schizoid aloofness coexists with extreme identification with his country.
Both qualities are pathological in normal times but necessary and advan-
tageous in crisis. 'Taking refuge abroad', wrote François Mauriac, 'a
madman imagined he was France, and the world believed him because it
was true, because his assertion, which appeared to be that of a madman,
actually proceeded from an analysis of reality' (p. 13).

Mutual identification of charismatic leader and nation is clear also in
the life and career of David Ben-Gurion, one of the founding fathers of
the State of Israel and its first Prime Minister. In Ben-Gurion's case,
childhood trauma strongly affected this identification. According to his

biographer Shabtai Teveth (1987), the death of his mother when he was ten was decisive in his political career. His lifelong sense of loss gave him the conviction to express with rare force the yearning and anger of a people who had lost their motherland and to lead their struggle to rebuild their ancestral homeland.* Teveth writes of this trait as a handicap in Ben-Gurion's personal life but a major asset in his political life, for his abstract idealization of his dead mother 'lay behind his feeling, never explicitly expressed, that he and the Zionist movement, or he and the Jewish people, were one and the same' (p. 11).

In normal times, such patriotic identification with one's people or country may be dismissed as 'the last refuge of a scoundrel', a futile escape from grief and alienation or from other unresolved personal problems, transparently an inappropriate projection of an inner world on to a very different public arena. In crisis, public critical judgement is often suspended, and what is seen is not the 'madman' described by Mauriac but an adulated saviour, expert in resolving crisis or turning it to advantage. By becoming a public being, the charismatic may find the resolution, the love and wholeness which were lost, attenuated or never had in private life.

The appearance of being one and the same with their nation is a fundamental trait of the great charismatics and is yet another link with mystics. Yet it is largely illusory. The yearning for union is often coupled, in a not-unsurprising paradox, with a sense of being alien. Robespierre, Lenin and Mussolini, for example, spoke for the masses of working people, but did not belong to them. Napoleon, born in Corsica of Italian origin, had faulty French. Garibaldi, born in Nice, a French citizen, spoke clumsy Italian. Herzl, a secular Western European Jew, found the majority of his followers among East European Jews whose language, Yiddish, he hardly knew. Roosevelt, a patrician born to America's aristocracy with all advantages of birth and wealth, spoke in defence of the common man against the interests of big business. Hitler, Austrian-born, became a German citizen the year before he became Chancellor of Germany.

How is one to interpret this paradox of the alien or alienated charismatic at the same time becoming identified with a nation or people towards whom he is in many ways an outsider, but who is nevertheless accepted by the nation as its spokesman?

One explanation, which the coming chapters touch on and the conclusion elaborates, involves the alienation and uncertainty which crisis breeds. These forces may bond a country to a charismatic who has already

---

* A similar psychology apparently underlies the charismatic role of Bialik, as seen in Chapter 6 below.

encountered them on a private, psychological level, and has constructed defences against them. For as suggested previously, the crises which bring charismatics to power are not entirely new to them. These crises have far worse parallels in their former lives, which have prepared, toughened, in some cases fanaticized them. Just as in personal relationships, individuals repeat (or transfer) childhood patterns of behaviour and attitudes to the present (Freud and Breuer, 1895; Storr, 1979), so also, it seems, in the political relationship between the charismatic and the public or nation (Kets de Vries, in Conger and Kanungo, eds., 1988, pp. 237–52; Aberbach, 1995). Political crisis may in some charismatics revive unresolved personal crisis. It can offer a second chance, as it were, a means of abreaction* and symbolic resolution. In childhood crisis, the charismatic-to-be is overwhelmed by unfamiliar, uncontrollable circumstances. This time he is – or tries to be, or to appear to be – ready and in control. For example, the violent upheaval of 1789 was not totally new to Robespierre. His life between 1764, when his mother died, and 1772, when his father disappeared for good, was a figurative reign of terror. Nor was the nature of the American Civil War entirely new to Lincoln. He knew from bitter experience what it meant to live in a house divided. It may be imagined that among the effects of his mother's death when he was nine was inner conflict – between anger and idealization, destructiveness and the longing for union and harmony. Nor were the emotions evoked by the Russian Revolution new to Lenin. The chaos, upheaval and violence were familiar to him, on a personal level, from the time of his father's death and his brother's execution thirty years previously.

Such personal crises help to explain why public crises which defeat others are often greeted with exhilaration by charismatic leaders. They see in crisis, perhaps unconsciously, opportunities to find outlets, mostly symbolic, for the resolution of their otherwise unresolvable inner disabilities. The immense benefits to a society from such psychological drives are more immediately apparent than the equally powerful dangers.

That the charismatic's handling of the crisis which leads to power might reflect an earlier, private schooling in crisis is unusually clear in the life of Franklin D. Roosevelt. Roosevelt was crippled by polio in 1921 at the age of thirty-nine. When asked about the impact of this illness on Roosevelt's life and career, his wife Eleanor replied: 'Anyone who has gone through great suffering is bound to have a greater sympathy and understanding of the problems of mankind' (Morgan, 1985, p. 259). Roosevelt

---

* A psychological term which refers to the discharge of blocked emotion attached to repressed experiences, relationships and thoughts.

spent his last twenty-four years without use of his legs. The spiritual battle against his affliction was at the core of his charismatic appeal as president of the United States during the Depression and World War II. Prior to his illness, he served as assistant secretary to the Navy. His salient qualities then often appeared to be the negative ones. He could be, and often was, arrogant, vain, self-serving, devious, disloyal and publicity-seeking. In the pre-1921 period, according to his biographer Ted Morgan, 'He knew nothing about labour, and wasn't interested' (*ibid.*, p. 126). Then came the so-called Newport Scandal in which Roosevelt was exposed as the Navy official responsible for recruiting newly-enlisted sailors to trap homosexuals by having sex with them. A Senate subcommitte concluded in a report released in late July 1921 that Roosevelt had lied about his involvement and had shown a total lack of moral perspective. This revelation 'was literally a crippling blow' (*ibid.*, p. 250): within three weeks, his resistance lowered by the shock, he came down with polio and was paralyzed.

Roosevelt fought the effects of his illness. He refused to accept defeat and learned from adversity. His passage from despair to hope changed him from being a shallow, ambitious, somewhat unscrupulous politician into a leader of great spiritual strength. When faced with disaster in the 1930s, America had a leader who had already faced and overcome personal disaster. To Roosevelt, the idea of 'running' for office and leading the nation out of a 'crippling' depression was symbolic of victory over private infirmity. He compared the nation to a body and social inequity to illness which could be healed through effective government. He used the idea of paralysis as a symbol in his inaugural address of 4 March 1933 – 'The only thing we have to fear is fear itself – nameless, unreasoning, unjustified terror which paralyzes needed efforts to convert retreat into advance' – a statement upon which Morgan elaborates:

> Roosevelt's transformation through debilitating illness was analogous to the situation of the country. In the twelve years of Republican rule that just about coincided with the period of his illness and attempted rehabilitation, the country went from health and prosperity to illness and breakdown. His predicament seemed to be a private expression of the state of the nation, crippled by depression and unemployment, its motor cells destroyed . . . His illness made it possible for him to identify with the humiliations and defeats of depression America. It was a suffering land, but it had the capacity to change and to grow, as he did. Indeed, this capacity for growth became the core of his character (*ibid.*, pp. 261, 771).

The charisma of John F. Kennedy was similarly, though less clearly, dependent on the intersection of private disability and exceptional gifts with public need. In his biography of Kennedy, Nigel Hamilton (1992) argues that Kennedy's emotional detachment and his struggle for inner freedom after an emotionally crippling childhood were the mainspring of his political career and his appeal, especially to women. The absence of a warm and loving family life made public life exceptionally attractive to Kennedy, who in any case was born into a family of politicians and had politics in his blood. Hamilton points out (p. 81) that Kennedy's experience of neglect as a child was in fact not atypical of 19th and early 20th century aristocratic families, such as Churchill's, in which social standing and climbing were an obsession. This neglect was greatly exacerbated, however, by an unusual number of other factors: the size of Kennedy's family – there were eight other children, including a retarded younger sister; his parents' apparently loveless marriage, fatally undermined by suppressed mutual hostility; their frequent absenteeism, each going separate ways, leaving the children to be raised by nannies, nurses, caretakers and by one another. There was also Kennedy's extraordinary medical history, a series of often-mysterious and, one suspects, at times partly psychosomatic illnesses in childhood (and onward until his death), including one three-month separation from his family recuperating from scarlet fever.

Most importantly, the character of his parents evidently left lasting wounds which indirectly became among the determining forces of Kennedy's political being. His mother, though fervently religious, was emotionally cold, an 'Ice Maiden' who treated her family as a factory to be managed (p. 44). She never kissed or touched her children and rarely saw them. In her priggish insistence on correct manners, discipline, and the suppression of emotion, she turned the family home into an 'orphanage'. Kennedy was sent from home at age thirteen to a boarding school where he spent four gruelling years during which his mother (like Churchill's mother) never visited (p. 96).

In Hamilton's view, Kennedy absorbed this coldness and the sense of deprivation, which pervaded both his private and public life:

He would never wholly overcome his sense of abandonment and maternal deprivation, which would condemn him to a lifetime's fruitless romantic and sexual searching . . . His mother's coldness and preoccupation with jewelry, clothes, and grooming gave him a lifelong aversion to such sexless artifices [as normal gestures of affection], as he buried his fractured psyche in a lifetime of fruitless womanizing, of continual, purgative sexual conquest that would relieve his libido yet never bring him contentment. Except in sexual excitement he hated to be touched, hated the very idea of loving attachment to a woman involving lasting commitment or affection (pp. 49–50, 112–13).

Kennedy's experience of maternal deprivation created in him a narcissistic hunger for public adulation. He became a Don Juan politically as well as sexually:

> His narcissistic personality craved success – social, sexual, professional. Deprived of early maternal warmth, he wanted attention, adulation, affection . . . his love of politics reflected his love life: an unwillingness to either surrender his obsession or surrender to it (pp. 380, 451).

His emotional detachment, a liability in personal relationships, allowed him a protean adaptability in public life. He became the first American president to understand fully and master the media, willingly becoming a media commodity – 'We'll sell him like soap flakes', his father once said. He consciously created a mythic persona, using external events, policies and actions not for their own sakes alone but as part of a process of self-creation in the dramaturgy of high office. By splitting public self from private self, he remained detached from virtually all issues in political life and was notably cool in crisis. In this way, he adapted himself wholly and without scruple to the goals of political power, influence and fame.

And indeed, Kennedy succeeded in gaining the sort of adulation usually reserved for dictators or pop stars. Untouched in childhood and hating the touch of affection, he touched the masses. The crowds that gathered for Kennedy in 1960, writes Theodore H. White (1962), were spectacular in their frenzy (p. 330). Especially after Kennedy's televised debates with Richard Nixon, he aroused immense excitement, at times bordering on worship, mainly among his female 'jumpers', 'leapers', 'clutchers', 'touchers', 'squeezers', 'screamers', and 'runners'. Such behaviour, unprecedented in American presidential campaigns, has many parallels among media charismatics who suffered parallel forms of deprivation in childhood; and it may be that the response to Kennedy's appeal, similarly, involved a subliminal longing to compensate him for this deprivation.

While Kennedy's mother blocked him emotionally, his father, according to Thomas C. Reeves (1991), nurtured in him fundamental flaws in character. Kennedy was deficient in integrity, compassion and tolerance. His failings endangered the welfare of the country and of the free world, demeaned the presidency and made him vulnerable to blackmail. In no American president was there a greater gap between the ideal image created by the media and the reality, which included countless sexual improprieties, sordid Mafia involvements, shady election tactics and vote fraud, and various forms of dishonesty concerning his intellectual achievements, his war record, the degree of his father's political and financial influence on him, his physical condition and his marriage.

Yet, writes Hamilton, there was one principle in which Kennedy apparently did believe – freedom; and it may be that his commitment to the ideal of freedom derived in part from his frustrated longing to break away from his father's lifelong influence. Kennedy's father was by all accounts a ruthless tyrant, a self-made multi-millionaire, hard, mean, irascible, selfish, oppressive, frightening, amoral – he was in the habit of humiliating his wife by bringing his mistresses home. He was also manipulative and often demeaning, highly ambitious, competitive and demanding. Kennedy's father bankrolled his political career, often far outspending his rivals in legitimate expenses as well as in bribes, payoffs and hush money.

Kennedy might have become president without this powerful support – he had ample talent and ambition. Yet he never shook free of feeling that his father ran his life; that he was imprisoned, even enslaved, and was constantly watched by him; that he was, in effect, an instrument of his father's revenge, as a once-scorned Irish Catholic, on the WASP establishment which the family fought to enter; and a tool of his father's unrealized ambitions for high office. In the view of a number of scholars, including Hamilton and Reeves, Kennedy lacked real depth, seriousness of purpose and commitment. Only the idea of freedom aroused strong feeling in him. Freedom was 'the key to Jack's political heart' (p. 791), the only plank in his political philosophy – if he had one. As a result, his passionate opposition to the abuses of communism had the ring of truth: 'in its threat to "freedom," the Soviet menace touched an area of Jack's own psyche where he was most sensitive . . .' and he became 'the West's most committed anti-Soviet freedom fighter, willing to risk even nuclear war rather than submit to the dictates of "a small clique of ruthless, powerful and selfish men" running a "slave state"' (pp. 789, 791). The force of this conviction, Hamilton writes, came partly out of Kennedy's struggle to preserve his own inner freedom in the shadow of his 'Stalinesque' father, towards whom he was invariably servile (pp. 790–1). He once described his father's relationship with him as that of ventriloquist and dummy (Collier and Horowitz, 1984, p. 162).

Dealing with Khrushchev, Kennedy said, was like dealing with his father – 'all give and no take' (*ibid.*, p. 277). His subservience and weakness *vis-à-vis* his father and father-figures was evidently sensed by the Russians. In part because they were convinced that Kennedy was a weak president, the Russians were encouraged to test American strength and resolve in the Berlin crisis of 1961 and the Cuban crisis of 1962. In both instances, Kennedy showed exceptional qualities of leadership and courage in the defence of freedom.

It is, nevertheless, an irony of American political history that Kennedy's

murder may have saved him from blackmail, ignominy and even impeach-
ment, making almost obligatory the creation of a romantic idealistic myth
and achieving symbolically for Kennedy in death something he never had
in his lifetime: the warm and loving embrace of a nation and of the free
world.

To sum up: charisma is defined as a dynamic force whose essence is the
dialectic of paradox. It is the creative clash and embrace of inner fantasy
and political reality. Though deeply personal and individual – at times
dictatorial – charisma has nevertheless helped to shape most of the major
modern democracies. It creates and is created by crisis. The charismatic is
often an alien, from a broken or distorted family background, yet up to a
point can create a group sense of familial harmony and unity. The charismatic is weak and ordinary as well as powerful and exceptional. He may
need social chaos to come to power but has utter faith that an orderly
Destiny has chosen him. He creates a persona disguising his true self, but
this persona becomes real. He leads with magnetic power but also is led.
He appears to be known to a large public but his inner life is a mystery.
He is, at times, hailed ecstatically as a saviour, only to lead his followers
to disaster. The selfless dedication and idealism of the charismatic is a
form of selfishness. He obeys the law of political expediency while being
driven by irrational, at times even mystical, impulses.

The similarities between political and religious charismatic leadership
are considerable. Why this is so is discussed later. The next two chapters
take up motifs touched on so far: the ephemerality of charisma, its pathological side, and the intersection of the charismatic's inner life and political
reality.

2 Churchill in 1940–1: The Fragility of Charisma

'We are all worms. But I do believe that I am a glowworm.'

Churchill

Politically outcast in the 1930s, Winston Churchill was far from being a charismatic leader. Not long before he became Prime Minister, he was one of the least popular leaders in Britain. Only with the outbreak of war did he rise to power in two stages: first, when war was declared on 3 September 1939, to First Lord of the Admiralty; then, eight months later, to Prime Minister on the eve of the German invasion of France. Now, with virtually unanimous support in Parliament, Churchill was given a rapturous welcome wherever he went and treated at times almost as if he had talismanic qualities. His oratory which a few months before had been put down as the overblown antiquated ramblings of a man whose career as a politician had already ended in failure, now held Parliament in thrall. Rarely has the elusive nature of charisma been illustrated so dramatically. At this moment, and at this moment alone, Churchill and Britain found one another to be at one, and Churchill's inner world and motives and the national will coincided.

Whether or not Churchill's leadership was decisive in winning the war or, at any rate, in Britain's decision to fight on, is open to question. The military historian Basil Liddell Hart thought not, for although Churchill shone by his fighting spirit, 'The British have always been less dependent than other people upon inspiring leadership . . . in their case, inspiring leadership may be regarded as an additional asset rather than a necessity' (Taylor, ed., 1973, p. 187). Against this view is the fact that until the summer of 1940, there were still influential members of the British government, such as Lord Halifax, who were ready to negotiate a peace settlement with Germany. When Hitler made his peace offer to Britain on 19 July 1940, a leader less pugnacious and determined and less capable of inspiring the nation than Churchill – Halifax was the second choice for Prime Minister after Churchill – might have lost heart and succumbed.

17

A great shift in national morale was achieved by the first of Churchill's great speeches in the Commons on 13 May 1940, three days after he became Prime Minister. In this speech, Churchill set the tone for Britain's conduct during the war:

> I have nothing to offer but blood, toil, tears and sweat . . . You ask, what is our policy? I can only say: It is to wage war by sea, land and air, with all our might and with all the strength that God can give us, to wage war against a monstrous tyranny, never surpassed in the dark, lamentable catalogue of human crime. That is our policy. You ask, what is our aim? I can answer in one word: It is victory, victory at all costs, victory in spite of all terror, victory however long and hard the road may be.

The historian Robert Rhodes James comments movingly on the impact of this speech:

> What will always be remembered as the 'blood, sweat and tears' speech was a real turning point. It stirred the Commons to its depths. It came to the British people as a call to service and sacrifice. It rang round the world, and thrilled the many friends of Western civilization with the realization that Britain was going to fight. There were those in 1940 who believed that Britain should seek a negotiated settlement with Hitler; perhaps it was, technically, the wisest thing to do. But after that first, unforgettable speech, such arguments lost whatever appeal they might have had. Here was the authentic voice of leadership and defiance. It was Churchill's outstanding quality as a war leader that he made the struggle seem not merely essential for national survival, but worthwhile and noble. No one – not even a child, as I was – who was in England in the summer of 1940 will ever forget the *cheerfulness* of the people. It was not even a gallows-humour mood. One caught Churchill's infectious spirit that this was a great time to be alive in; that Destiny had conferred a wonderful benefit upon us; and that these were thrilling days to live through. Of course, this mood could not be permanent, and the reality of sacrifice was a very different thing to the prospect. But the horror of war was to a remarkable extent exorcized by the exhilaration of the struggle, and I have no doubt that it was this that brought the British people through their ordeal (*ibid.*, pp. 108–9).

Even a revisionist historian such as Charmley (1993) acknowledges Churchill's strengths as a war leader: 'He realized the importance of emotion and symbols, and it was through their utilisation, via the medium of his oratory and the projection of his personality, that he galvanized the British people in 1940' (p. 465).*

Yet, Churchill's charismatic appeal in 1940–1 was not the result of any change in him, but in the British people. To Churchill, the horror of war had always counted less than the chivalry, the glory and the exhilaration of the struggle. As a child, his favourite toys were his huge collection of model soldiers with which he would recreate the military feats of his distinguished ancestor, the Duke of Marlborough. As a young war correspondent and soldier at the turn of the century, he courted danger in Cuba, on India's northwest frontier, on the Nile and in South Africa. His lust for adventure, excitement and glory was not unusual among young men of his class in the late Victorian and Edwardian eras. Yet his longing to be in the thick of battle and his fascination with weaponry and strategy were lifelong, persisting even when war was not fashionable. After falling from power as First Lord of the Admiralty in 1915 as a result of the disastrous invasion of the Dardanelles, Churchill enlisted as a front-line officer. He was then forty, with a wife and two small children. Later, as Minister of Munitions in the Lloyd George war government, he often flew to the Western front, needlessly exposing himself to injury and death. He was not one to run for shelter from flying shells and bullets. Rather, he enjoyed the sounds and sights of the war and wanted to be where the action was. 'I love the bangs', he said (Taylor, p. 157). During one such visit to the front he was almost killed by an exploding shell. He wrote to his wife at the time that a difference of a few feet would have meant 'an impoverishment of the war-making power of Britain which no one would ever know or measure or mourn' (Gilbert, 1983, VI 314).

Such belligerence was anathema to Britain after the slaughter of World War I. Churchill's outlook and style were seen as anachronistic for much of the decade after his resignation from the cabinet in 1931. During the 1930s, Churchill *lacked* charisma precisely because he needed and loved the unavailable drug of war. He was aware that his happiness in wartime was an abnormality, confessing to his wife on the eve of the 1914–18 war: 'Everything tends towards catastrophe and collapse. I am interested, geared up and happy. Is it not horrible to be built like that?' (*ibid.*, 1971, III 80). As for World War II, he said that 1940 and 1941 were the best

---

* Ponting (1994, p. 455ff.), however, plays down the impact of Churchill's oratory. Both Charmley and Ponting emphasize Britain's decision under Churchill to fight Germany in 1940 as the death blow to the British empire rather than as a heroic battle against the evil of Nazism. This emphasis has been attacked by other historians as a distorted reading of history.

years of his life. In common with other charismatic political leaders, such as Robespierre, Lenin and Hitler, he felt that Destiny had chosen him for this hour and that his past life had been but a preparation for the trial of standing alone against Hitler (*ibid.*, 1983, VI 317).

In the fight against Hitler, Churchill who prior to the war had seemed an old man on the verge of retirement – he was sixty-four when the war broke out – now gained a new lease on life. His spirits soared and his friend Brendan Bracken who had known him for nearly twenty years said that he had never seen Churchill as fit as he was in 1940 (*ibid.*, p. 670). He was an unceasing fount of aggressive energy, inspiration and offensive plans, as Ian Jacob of his Defence Office recalled: 'His pugnacious spirit demanded constant action. The enemy must be assailed continuously: the Germans must be made to "bleed and burn"' (*ibid.*, p. 326).

Churchill's disregard for his own safety was as much in evidence during World War II as it had been in his early years. He could not resist climbing to the roof of 10 Downing Street to watch the German air attacks at the height of the Battle of Britain. Characteristically, not until the worst of the London Blitz was over did he bow to pressure and transfer his working headquarters and bedroom to a proper shelter near Downing Street. Also typical were Churchill's disappointment and chagrin at not being allowed to go with the troops on D Day, instead arriving in Normandy several days after the invasion began.

Churchill's unusually intense love of war and his tempting of death were essential ingredients of his charisma in 1940–1. For the first and only time in his life, his character and the needs of the British people were in harmony: for what was required was a leader of uncompromising, fearless, even reckless, courage.

Churchill's readiness for self-sacrifice was apparently born not just out of a conviction of being saved by Destiny for a great role. It also came from a chronic lack of self-esteem and a profound feeling of personal worthlessness, for which the sense of being chosen was perhaps a compensation. His quest for danger might also have expressed a secret wish for death. For long periods in his life he suffered deep depression, his 'Black Dog' (Storr, in Taylor, ed.). He confessed to his doctor, Lord Moran, that there were times when he feared that he might commit suicide. At these times, he would take precautions. For example, he would avoid standing on the edge of a railway platform as the train was coming in or by the rail of a ship looking down into the water (Moran, 1966, p. 167). Brendan Bracken described him as a 'despairer'. His self-esteem was bound up with success in public, rather than private, life. When he was out of office, after the Dardanelles fiasco and during the 1930s, he was plunged into despair, certain that he was 'finished' (*ibid.*, p. 745). At the end of his life, he confessed to his daughter Diana that 'I have achieved a great deal to achieve nothing in the end' (S. Churchill, 1967, p. 17).

The psychiatrist Anthony Storr (in Taylor, ed.) has suggested that Churchill's depressive bent inclined him to polymathic activities as a strategy for fighting the Black Dog. Most importantly, there was his political career which extended over sixty years, during which he held most of the major positions in government. In addition, he wrote over fifty books, including two mammoth histories of the world wars and biographies of his ancestor, the Duke of Marlborough, and of his father, Lord Randolph Churchill. His intense, persistent search for excitement, for the thunder of war and for heroic adventure at the risk of life was, perhaps, Churchill's strongest defence against the Black Dog. He was also drawn to the colour and power of language and oratory – he is the only world statesman to have won the Nobel Prize for Literature – as well as to colourful hobbies, such as collecting butterflies and tropical fish and painting in bright colours. The lively, extravert type of friend to which he was attracted, such as Lord Birkenhead (F.E. Scott), Lord Beaverbrook and Brendan Bracken, was also an antidote to despair. Churchill's activities, taken separately, cannot be attributed to the one defensive aim. Yet the general extent and vigour of his activities certainly had the effect of keeping depression at bay.

How might these alleged defences against the Black Dog be linked with Churchill's charisma in 1940–1? Churchill's appeal may have sprung largely from his ability, built up in the course of a lifetime's battle against depression, to make use of external stimulus in order to overcome despair, of which Storr writes: 'In 1940, any political leader might have tried to rally Britain with brave words, although his heart was full of despair. But only a man who had known and faced despair within himself could carry conviction at such a moment' (Taylor, ed., p. 206). Churchill's speeches during the war are full of the aggressive insistence that in the darkest crisis, fortitude and courage would lead to eventual victory. When he said that the sorrow and the suffering themselves would provide the means of survival, he might have been speaking of his own inner state. In a broadcast of 11 September 1940, at the height of the London Blitz, he declared that 'we shall draw from the heart of suffering itself the means of inspiration and survival' (Gilbert, 1983, VI 779). In the following year, in a broadcast of 12 June 1941, he offered a similarly prophetic message of hope: 'All will come right. Out of the depths of sorrow and sacrifice will be born again the glory of mankind' (*ibid.*, p. 1109).

Storr's interpretation of Churchill's character does not deal specifically with charisma, but his argument is applicable to the general nature of charisma as a possible response to parental deprivation or distortion. Storr argues that while Churchill's depressive nature – his Black Dog – might have been partly hereditary, it was probably also a result of serious childhood neglect. Churchill's son, Randolph, wrote of him: 'The neglect and lack of interest in him shown by his parents were remarkable even by the standards of late Victorian and Edwardian days' (1966, p. 43). Churchill's mother, Jennie, though warm, vivacious and highly intelligent, was preoccupied by a ceaseless whirl of socializing and had little time for him. His father, Lord Randolph Churchill, had his political career – he rose to the position of Chancellor of the Exchequer – which, likewise, left him with little time for his son whom he seems to have disliked. A tragic, suppressed element in the relationship, or the lack of one, between father and son was that Randolph had syphilis. He died from this disease when Churchill was twenty. Churchill discovered the true nature of his father's illness only a few weeks before the latter's death. It may be that his father kept him at a distance for reasons having to do with his disease. Not surprisingly, Churchill retained longstanding bitterness towards his father: 'I owe everything to my mother', he said, 'to my father nothing' (Harris, 1920, p. 92).

Churchill was virtually abandoned by his parents in infancy. He was raised by a nanny, Mrs. Everest, who was his closest friend and confidant throughout his childhood and early manhood (her picture hung in his room until he died). At Harrow, where he spent four and a half years, he was hardly ever visited by his parents. In his letters he constantly begged them to come. His poor behaviour at this time might have expressed protest at this neglect. The epithets frequently used by his teachers to describe him might also describe his own, perhaps unconscious, hostility to his parents, uncoloured by bias: 'troublesome', 'very bad', 'careless', 'very naughty'.

As a result, writes Storr, Churchill apparently failed to develop a firm inner sense of self-esteem and was exceptionally prone to depression. Deprivation fueled his compulsive ambition and his dependence upon external sources of self-esteem, such as success in political life. It also made him liable to compensatory fantasies of being special and of having a heroic mission. In battling the potential sources of weakness in him, Churchill built up formidable inner strength and courage. Churchill's aggressive defiance is immortalized in lines such as those spoken in the House of Commons on 4 June 1940:

> We shall not flag or fail. We shall fight in France, we shall fight on the
> seas and oceans, we shall fight with growing confidence and growing

strength in the air, we shall defend our island, whatever the cost may be, we shall fight on the beaches, we shall fight on the landing grounds, we shall fight in the fields and in the streets, we shall fight in the hills, we shall never surrender.

This belligerent style was often a liability in war as in peace and, as indicated earlier, in the 1930s had been unpopular. Yet in 1940, for once, Churchill's aggressiveness could be given full rein against a legitimate demonic target. The intensity of this hostility, in Storr's view, was related to Churchill's emotional deprivation in childhood and to the depression which subsequently plagued him:

> The emotionally deprived child who later becomes prey to depression has enormous difficulty in the disposal of his hostility. He resents those who have deprived him, but he cannot afford to show this resentment, since he needs the very people he resents; and any hostility he does manifest results in still further deprivation of the approval and affection he so much requires. In periods of depression, this hostility becomes turned against the self, with the result that the depressive under-values himself or even alleges that he is worthless: 'I have achieved a great deal to achieve nothing in the end.' It is this difficulty in disposing of hostility which drives some depressives to seek for opponents in the external world. It is a great relief to find an enemy on whom it is justified to lavish wrath . . . when [Churchill] was finally confronted by an enemy whom he felt to be wholly evil, it was a release which gave him enormous vitality. Hitler was such an enemy; and it is probable that Churchill was never happier than when he was fully engaged in bringing about Hitler's destruction (Taylor, ed., pp. 231–2).

Storr anticipates the criticism that any argument of this kind applied to such a great man as Churchill might easily be trivialized and dismissed as futile and impertinent. Black Dog sufferers do not inevitably become Churchills. Storr emphasizes that although Churchill has become a universal symbol of defiant bravery, he was also a human being. To draw attention to Churchill's humanity, to his flaws as well as to his inordinate strengths, in no way detracts from his achievements. His charismatic power appears to have been born out of a mixture of these weaknesses and strengths.

Just as good and evil sometimes counterpart one another, so also Churchill and Hitler, in the eyes of some historians, such as William Manchester (1983, 1988), were mirror images of each other; and the nature of their charismatic appeal has much in common. Although Churchill in the 1930s stood virtually alone in Parliament in warning of the dangers of Hitler and

Nazism, he also, up to a point, admired Hitler: he expressed the hope that if Britain were defeated in war as Germany had been in 1918, she too would have a revivalist leader of Hitler's stature (*ibid.*, 1983, p. 87). Both Churchill and Hitler have been described by psychologists as men who, to a marked degree, went against their own natures. Both were driven by the conviction of being chosen by Destiny and were fully identified with their respective countries. Sharing the belief that man's nobility is best expressed in war, both were jubilant at the outbreak of war and, in battle, showed exceptional bravery under fire. Artists by temperament – both painted – they were guided by instinct rather than by reason. Lloyd George once compared Churchill to an apparently sane chauffeur who drives with great skill for a few months, then suddenly without warning takes the car off a cliff. Under the pressure of war, Churchill, too, showed signs of despotism and megalomania, though he was curbed from his more extreme impulses by his war cabinet and his generals. Like Hitler, Churchill depended for his appeal on oratory. In conversation they both tended to soliloquize and to dominate their listeners. Both were deeply troubled by distortions in family background, having suffered hostility at the hands of their fathers and greatly idealizing their mothers; both were driven to seek sources of self-esteem in public life. Both were prone to depression and needed an enemy: Hitler found his in the Jews; Churchill, in Hitler. Yet, whereas Churchill was a saviour of the free world, Hitler was a cold-blooded tyrant, the murderer of millions of innocent civilians, the incarnation and byword of evil.

Churchill's gifts as a war leader far exceeded his abilities as a leader in peacetime. His appeal did not survive the war. For a short period, his lifelong battle against inner demons found an external counterpart in the fight against Hitler. In this intersection between inner conflict and political crisis, Churchill found a temporary niche as charismatic leader of genius in Britain's darkest hour.

3 Hitler: Charisma and Racism

'... die treuste Liebe
trog keiner wie er!'
Wagner, *Götterdämmerung*

Hitler came to power through an extraordinary concatenation of political and economic crisis, personal gifts and psychopathology. The historical circumstances which paved the way for Hitler have been studied extensively, and Hitler's family background has been explored as far as the meagre documentation allows (e.g. Bullock, 1986; Fest, 1974; Toland, 1977; Flood, 1989). Yet, the undoubted vital interconnection between Hitler's charismatic power as a political leader and his inner world remains obscure.

The historical facts are not in dispute: Germany's defeat in World War I, the unprecedented, futile suffering and death, the uncertainty, frustration and rage, the blow to national pride, made possible Hitler's entry to politics. Germany's traditional problems – *Lebensraum* and unity – became national obsessions after the war, especially as the Russian Revolution threatened to spill over into Germany. Amid panic, disunity, and political and economic upheaval, Hitler took his first steps to power. The Wall Street crash of 1929, and the panic and depression which followed, precipitated his ascent to the Chancellorship. In the 1928 elections, Hitler's party had received 811,000 votes (about 100,000 less than in 1926); in 1930, 6.3 million Germans voted for him.

Hitler came to power in 1933 through democratic means, with the support of the masses. He was welcomed by intellectuals as well as workers, by industrialists and artists, farmers and philosophers, generals and housewives. Many considered him to be a charming, intelligent, perceptive, highly competent and many-sided leader – a born politician. His achievements until the War were not inconsiderable. He eliminated unemployment through a massive rearmament programme (there were six million unemployed when he came to power), stabilized the currency, provided effective social legislation, and gave Germany for the first time since 1914 a sense of unity and optimism.

Despite the purges of the SA and the Nuremburg Laws of 1935, David

Lloyd-George could describe Hitler as 'the George Washington of Germany'; and Churchill, while warning against Hitler, was deeply impressed by his accomplishments until 1937. And in the 1930s the German people willingly, even joyfully, pledged their loyalty not merely to Hitler the politician but to Hitler the myth, the semi-deity, the Messiah, the embodiment of the national will. Never in history has one man wielded such charismatic power over a people.

How can Hitler's hold on the German people be explained? Part of the answer lies in Alan Bullock's observation that no political leader has ever shown greater understanding of the irrational and emotional factors in politics, or exploited them more masterfully. Hitler's instinct for the theatrical – Chaplin once described him as 'the greatest actor of us all' (Chaplin Jnr., 1960, p. 204) – his fanatically sincere oratory, his use of his hands and eyes (for which he received professional training), hypnotized his audiences and brought about their complete identification with him. In a broader perspective, however, Isaiah Berlin has pointed out, 'there is no such thing as long-lived mass hypnotism; the masses know what it is that they like, what genuinely appeals to them. What the Germans thought Hitler to be, Hitler, in fact, largely was . . .' (1982, p. 29).

Bryan Wilson has described Hitler as the last political leader to succeed through unrestrained appeal to the primitive, romantic, and atavistic passions of men, through the 'rhetoric of charisma' which

> employs an earthy vocabulary of body imagery and basic biological elements. In these terms the in-group is reassured of itself and its boundaries, and its being as a 'natural' entity. It is no accident that Hitler's ideological repertoire drew so heavily on race, blood, ruralism, primitive native virtue, pre-Christian religious imagery, folk values, and semi-mystical atavism (1975, p. 105).

This most primitive appeal was made by means of the most sophisticated technology of the age. Hitler was the first master of the mass media, of radio and the newsreel (sound came in just as his career was about to take off), and of the modern election campaign (Kershaw, 1987, 1991). The newness of it all gave his presence and voice in mass rallies an almost apocalyptic quality. His propaganda was planned and carried out with utmost effectiveness. Such forces seem to have overwhelmed the German masses, raised in a highly authoritarian family structure, social hierarchy, educational system and military tradition. Tens of thousands of ex-servicemen who had not found a place in post-War German society were magnetized by Hitler; he was, after all, one of them, and he offered them a uniform, a group identity and an outlet for their frustrations. Their resistance lowered by the terror of political and economic chaos, by a lingering sense of inferiority, betrayal and hate, Germans were on the whole willing to throw their lot in with Hitler and ignore the possibility of disastrous long-term consequences.

The short-term gains were considerable. Hitler's violent assumption of dictatorial power in 1933–4 gave Germany unity; his persecution of the Jews and the Nuremberg Laws assuaged German inferiority; the repudiation of the terms of the Versailles Treaty and the military build-up alleviated German shame at being defeated; the remilitarization of the Rhineland (1936), the 'bloodless conquests' of Austria and the Sudetenland (1938) and Czechoslovakia (1939) reinforced Germany's new-found sense of power and vitality.

The price that the world paid in the end was over 35 million dead; and the price paid by Germany was defeat and the stigma of having dehumanized itself by criminally dehumanizing and murdering countless victims.

Who was Hitler? What were the inner sources of his charisma and of his murderous hatred, particularly of the Jews? The fullest account of Hitler's early life appears in John Toland's biography. Hitler's father was an Austrian customs official who never knew his father (who might have been a Jew) and who lost his mother in childhood. He was a brutal, tyrannous man and led a stormy marital life. A niece whom he first adopted and later married (after the deaths of his first two wives) became Hitler's mother. After losing three children, she gave birth to Hitler in 1889. The bond between mother and son was unusually close and protective as she feared losing him as she had lost her other children, and also because of her husband's harsh character and the age difference between them – she was twenty-three years younger than he.

The mother's loving tenderness contrasting with the father's cruelty and rages (he frequently beat his son) might be reflected in the split between Hitler's later idealization of Germany in *Mein Kampf* as the 'faithful mother' and his condemnation of Austria as a traitorous father-figure, guilty, among other things, of sexual immorality, incestuous and Jewish (Langer, 1972). (Hitler's father, in contrast, was proud of being Austrian and regarded being called *einer Deutscher*, a German, an insult.)

Even if Hitler's father was not part-Jewish, Hitler apparently came to suspect that he was. The intensity of his later anti-Semitism might, therefore, have sprung partly from his hatred of – and identification with – what he perceived his father and himself as being. Also, the loss of his older siblings and of a younger brother who died when he was about eleven might have predisposed him to a later feeling of being chosen, infallible and invincible (*ibid.*). (Stalin also lost three siblings [Deutscher, 1989]; and he and Hitler were together responsible for the deaths of some eighty million human beings [Bullock, 1991]). It may be that Hitler's alleged monorchism – the Russian autopsy report revealed that one of his testicles had not descended – intensified the pathological tendencies created by tensions within his family (Waite, 1977).

Other characteristics of Hitler in later life, which served to fuel his charismatic power, might also be related to his family structure. His mother's overly-close, anxious attachment to him might have contributed to his later aversion to normal heterosexual relations (he said that he was 'married' to Germany) and the repudiation of his 'feminine' softness, weakness and fear (he suffered from innumerable phobias) in favour of an extreme masculine ideal of toughness and brutality. His relationship to the German masses, as he saw it, was one of man to woman, and it might have involved a displaced incestuous attachment to his mother. Psychologists have suggested that the charismatic union which he established with his audiences represented a constant renewal of his symbiotic tie with his mother (Carr, 1978).

Leaving such conjectures aside, the deaths of Hitler's parents when he was in his teens were doubtless crucial in the growth of his psychopathology. His reaction to his father's sudden death in 1903 is unknown, but apart from grief, it might have included an element of relief at being rid of a tyrant and guilt at having wanted his death. The death of his mother, however, was perhaps the greatest blow in his life. She died slowly of cancer in 1907, and Hitler nursed her during her last two months. Her doctor was a Jew, Eduard Bloch, who used the primitive, largely ineffectual, evil-smelling treatments then available.

It is believed by some psychologists (e.g. Bowlby, 1980) that the pathological nature of Hitler's hatred of the Jews, which was an integral part of his charismatic personality, might be linked with the hatred which the bereaved often feels towards the doctors of the lost person. In his speeches, Hitler frequently referred to the Jews as a stench-ridden cancer which had to be cut out if mother-Germany was to be saved. Also, he joined an anti-Semitic society several months after his mother's death. Dr. Bloch recalled thirty years later: 'In all my career I never saw anyone so prostrate with grief as Adolf Hitler' (Toland, p. 36). Hitler's periodic depressions in later life, during which he would contemplate or even threaten suicide, might ultimately be traced, in part at least, to the intensity of his bond with his mother and the manner of her death.

Hitler's failure to gain admission to the Academy of Fine Arts in Vienna, which he later blamed on Jewish influence, was a further severe blow. He spent the next few years as a down-and-out in Vienna hostels, earning a meagre livelihood from his paintings, sketches and posters. This existence seems to have resulted less from the lack of prospects than from his broken emotional state after his mother's death.

Hitler's inability at this time and for the rest of his life to establish a loving relationship with a woman was brought about partly by his grief-ridden attachment to his mother. His relations with women were always tormented – six of the women with whom he was closely associated in later life either committed suicide or attempted to do so. According to Walter Langer's wartime report on Hitler for the American Secret Service, several informants reported that Hitler had a sexual perversion known as coprophilia: he gained sexual pleasure by having women defecate or urinate on him. In clinical cases, Robert Waite has pointed out in his study of Hitler, *The Psychopathic God*, this condition is invariably found in those with overwhelming feelings of inferiority, guilt and masochism, all of which played a vital part in Hitler's psychology and in the emergence within him of his opposite – the charismatic, omnipotent, brutally unprincipled *Führer*.

In pre-war Vienna, however, this persona had not yet formed, and those who knew Hitler at this time remembered that he looked more like a stereotype of a Jew than like an Aryan 'Superman'. He was an impoverished, shabby youth, in poor physical condition, insecure and excitable, living in his own world of fantasy, not lacking in intelligence and charm, and he had clearly been through a lot in life.

The hostels in which Hitler lived were supported by Jewish charities. It may be that the humiliation of having to undergo shower and disinfectant before entering was associated in Hitler's mind with the Jews and became part of the imagery of his later lust for revenge. At this time, however, he apparently did not use the Jews obsessionally as an outlet for his aggressions and frustrations, though he read popular anti-Semitic literature.

The outbreak of war in 1914 was a tremendous relief to him. In *Mein Kampf* he described how he fell to his knees and rapturously thanked Heaven for granting him the privilege of being alive at that time. He joined the German (not the Austro-Hungarian) army and was, by all accounts, obedient, loyal and brave under fire. Though he did not rise above the rank of corporal, he was awarded high military honours. In the fight for Germany, Hitler's apathy and depression seem to have vanished and were replaced by a sense of pride, security and belonging, as well as by an aim in life. The German army became a substitute for his broken family.

If there was a single point in Hitler's life when the 'psychopathic god' was born in him, when his relatively conventional problems, drives and prejudices crossed the border into dangerous insanity, that point was reached when Germany lost the War. At the time of Germany's surrender, Hitler was particularly susceptible to a psychotic reaction. In a mustard-gas attack in October 1918, he was blinded. For several weeks he lay in hospital recovering his sight. When news came of Germany's unexpected surrender, he went blind again (Toland, pp. xvi–xviii).

Hitler's gassing might have affected, if not directly brought about, his decision to exterminate the Jews by means of poison gas. Already in *Mein Kampf*, Hitler wrote:

> If at the beginning of the War and during the War, twelve or fifteen thousand of these Hebrew corruptors of the people had been held under poison gas, as happened to hundreds of thousands of our very best German workers in the field, the sacrifice of millions at the front would not have been in vain (quoted by Dawidowicz, 1983, p. 27).

At any rate, Hitler's blindness (which was afterwards used by German pathologists as a textbook case of hysteria) might be explained in psychological terms. For example, as Germany was equated in his mind with the 'faithful mother', her defeat might have revived the terrible grief which he felt on losing his mother; or that this defeat called up Hitler's alleged rage at his father for maltreating, perhaps sexually abusing, his mother. Whatever happened, a transformation took place inside Hitler which is of crucial importance in understanding the nature of his charismatic role: he heard visionary voices summoning him to liberate Germany and lead her to greatness. At this point, he claimed, his sight returned and he vowed to enter politics.

The work of Wilfred Bion (1961), himself a veteran of the War, on groups and leaders gives insight into the close links between Hitler's personal experiences and his charismatic appeal in Germany of the 1920s and 1930s. The War had caused loss of life on a scale unprecedented in history. In Germany, hardly a family did not have a father, a son, or a close relative killed or maimed. Post-war Germany was littered with broken families, cripples and bankrupts. Among Bion's various types of groups with different motives, one is particularly applicable to Germany: the basic assumption and oneness group which seeks a sense of well-being and unity. In such a group, the followers idolize the leader in order to overcome their fear of desertion. In a society wracked with bereavement and the humiliation of defeat as Germany was after 1918, the need for well-being and unity can become especially pressing, and can point the way to a dictatorship. For such a group, the natural leader may be one who has himself experienced severe loss and has developed inner defences by which to overcome the effects of grief and enable the masses to be fused into a collective unconscious (Lindholm, 1990). Hitler was such a leader.

Hitler was not just a politician but a visionary, the founder of a new religion, and his psychopathic qualities were an integral part of his charismatic appeal. His full-blown anti-Semitism apparently emerged shortly after the War, when 'international Jewry' was not infrequently blamed for Germany's defeat, for the Russian Revolution and the Communist threat. Lucy Dawidowicz, in *The War against the Jews 1933–45*, has shown how completely Hitler was a product of his environment:

> People living in an anti-Semitic *milieu* – as Hitler did – already viewed Jews as diseased and filthy creatures, degenerate and corrupting, outsiders beyond fraternity or compassion. Since the society had already branded the Jews as loathsome pariahs, the Jews could then serve the symbolic and pathological needs of the obsessed and the guilt-ridden (p. 34n).

Germany, in short, could be considered ripe for a psychopathic anti-Semitic ruler. The Church had always legitimized hatred of the Jews as the killers of Christ; German political leaders since Bismarck had used anti-Semitism as a political tool to gain power; popular German literature was full of virulently racist ideas which Hitler drew upon. When in 1920 the anti-Semitic forgery *The Protocols of the Elders of Zion* appeared in German, it sold 120,000 copies by the end of the year (*ibid.*, p. 77). Amid the insecurities and weak government of the post-War years, Germany looked for a strong leader and a scapegoat.

To a large extent, too, 19th century thinkers prepared the ground for Hitler and provided intellectual justification for his *Weltanschauung*. Apart from Richard Wagner, whose pathological hatred of the Jews had the utmost importance upon Hitler and the rise of Nazism (Osborne, 1977), other influences included Gobineau and the theory of Aryan superiority, Schopenhauer and his concept of the 'triumph of the will', and Nietzsche with his emphasis upon the will-to-power and upon violence as a cleansing force. Perhaps most important of all, however, was Darwin's doctrine of natural selection, which was taken to justify racism and the idea that might makes right, and which 'brought down one of the strongest barriers protecting "Thou shalt not kill"' (Talmon, in Sonntag, ed., 1980, p. 14). Of his experience in the 1914–18 war, Hitler wrote: 'I saw men falling around me in thousands. Thus I learned that life is a struggle and has no other object but the preservation of the species' (quoted by Toland, p. 936).

In Hitler's hands, the political, social and ideological norms were systematically pushed to their logical extremes, with the Jews as the main victims. 'Anti-Semitism', Lucy Dawidowicz has emphasized, 'was the core of Hitler's system of beliefs and the central motivation for his policies. He believed himself to be the saviour who would bring redemption to the German people through the annihilation of the Jews, that people who embodied, in his eyes, the Satanic hosts' (p. 208). Traditional suspicion, contempt and hatred of the Jews were turned by Hitler into mass paranoiac psychosis.

To read Hitler's account of the Jews in *Mein Kampf*, Alan Bullock has observed, is to enter the world of the insane. Yet, Hitler's dual image of the Jews as vermin to be exterminated and as a diabolical adversary was not uncommon in anti-Semitic literature. What was unusual was the sheer intensity of Hitler's hatred of the Jews, which became an end in itself rather than a means to an end. When he described the Jews as an 'emasculating germ . . . a parasite . . . bacillus . . . leech . . . vampire . . . fungus . . . cancer . . . tuberculosis' – he meant it. 'Only when we have eliminated the Jews', he wrote, 'will we regain our health.'

Emotionally crippled and perverse himself, surrounded by cripples, misfits and perverts, Hitler projected his self-image onto the Jews. He described the Jews as dictators, of mixed blood, who, while attempting to conquer the world, were engaging in genocide against the Aryan race. The Jews, to Hitler, were symbolic of 'the enemy within', of all that was both despicably weak and evilly omnipotent in him, and which threatened to engulf himself, Germany and the world.

Hitler must have genuinely believed that 'the Jews', sexually perverse and diseased, morally corrupt and pernicious, were to blame for Germany's lack of unity and *Lebensraum*, that they, in fact, had lost the war for Germany and, symbolically, had 'raped' the motherland. Communists, Socialists, Marxists, Democrats, Capitalists, and all his other enemies – including, in the end, Germany itself – were indiscriminately lumped together under the single rubric 'the Jews'. His 'holy mission', as he claimed in *Mein Kampf,* was 'in accordance with the will of the Almighty Creator: *by defending myself against the Jew, I am fighting for the work of the Lord.*'

Hitler gained the support of the German masses not because of his anti-Semitism as much as because he offered what was regarded as firm leadership in crisis. Yet, once he became Chancellor, the German people were, for the most part, willing to embrace or acquiesce in his anti-Semitic policies.

How did Hitler's pathology correspond with the state of post-War Germany to the point that he became virtually identified with Germany? The answer may lie in the transformation which he underwent in his speeches. He would usually begin nervously, uncertain and indecisive – the epitome of the German self-image in the wake of the 1914–18 debacle and the 1929 crash. In the course of his speeches, he would become transformed into his opposite: hard, brutal, all-powerful, capable of sadistic mass murder, heedless of conscience and guilt – *der Führer*. This transformation, which had an unmistakable sexual element, seems to have hypnotized his audiences and provoked in them an almost orgasmic reaction, for it expressed, in an extreme form, their own secret desire to be transformed, to be omnipotent and victorious. However, in order to convince himself that *der Führer* was real, Hitler continually had to suppress his natural uncertainties and indecisiveness, and to deny all weakness in him. In so doing, he committed himself to an increasingly radical path from which there was no retreat. 'No man was ever more surely destroyed by the image he had created', wrote Alan Bullock, 'than Adolf Hitler' (1986, p. 385). His conviction of god-like infallibility was a source both of his charismatic appeal and of his downfall. It is significant, perhaps, that the implementation of the Final Solution began in earnest in 1942, shortly after Hitler's first military reverses, when the image of the *Führer*'s invincibility had begun to fade. By this time it was apparent that Hitler was not primarily the enemy of the Jews, but of all mankind, including Germany.

The question remains: to what extent did Hitler create a National-Socialist Germany in his image, and to what extent was it the other way round? No doubt Hitler was at least partly mad. Who could conceive of monstrous Auschwitz unless, psychologically, Auschwitz was within him? Among the known factors, Hitler's background – the loss of several siblings, the distortions in his family life, the deaths of both parents when he was young – may well have predisposed him to pathological behaviour. World War I did the rest. Yet, even in his obsessive hatred of the Jews, Hitler appeared to be the epitome of sanity to a great many Germans, and this was at the heart of his charismatic appeal. Violent, unstable, self-destructive, Hitler was a creation and concave mirror-image of his country; and he came to power through the forceful correlation of his personal pathology with political crisis.

4 Charisma and Religion: From Ecstasy to Democracy

> 'He is their god. He leads them like a thing
> Made by some other deity than nature,
> That shapes man better; and they follow him
> Against us brats with no less confidence
> Than boys pursuing summer butterflies
> Or butchers killing flies . . .'
>
> *Coriolanus* IV vi 91–6

Only since the Reformation has industrial Western society come to distinguish sharply between religion and politics. Many less technologically advanced societies, in Africa or the Middle East for example, do not make this distinction. Charismatic movements in these regions, such as those of the Zulu messiah Isaiah Shembe, of Simon Mimbangu in the Belgian Congo or, more recently, of the Ayatollah Khomeini in Iran, do not separate the two. At the same time, no secular society is purely secular. Even the most advanced Western democracies have preserved or adapted elements of traditional religious authority as part of their political systems. The faiths and rituals of politics often contain more than a residual trace of religion. 'The secularization of society', writes Robert C. Tucker, 'does not so much mean the disappearance of religion as it does the weakening of the hold of religion *in its traditional forms*, along with the displacement of religious emotion into other areas, particularly the political' (1968, p. 733). For this reason, Tucker argues – and many sociologists and historians agree – Max Weber was right to extend the definition of charisma to the political sphere.

Weber posited a gradation of charisma from the ecstasy of primitive religion to the euphoria purveyed by the ethical prophet to the political passion stirred up by the charismatic union of leader and follower. However, there is no need to accept Weber's theoretical model in order to understand that religious charisma and political charisma are at times clearly linked. There are important differences: the great religious leaders and their claims are believed long after their deaths; and when the issue of

35

faith enters such comparisons, it throws into relief the erosion of charisma in modern political life. Also, political charisma is rooted in history, whereas religious charismatics and their followers invariably deny the purely historical and political thrust of their leadership. Instead, they emphasize the timeless ahistorical value of their sacred texts and religious message. History and biography are treated as subservient to a higher power, for on their own they may limit the value and credibility of the charismatic's authority.

Notwithstanding these differences, there is hardly a single element in the relationship between charismatic political leaders and their followers, and the background, character and aims of the political charismatic, that does not have a close parallel in religious charisma. Political charisma draws on the language, the spirit and even the ideological conviction of religion. Charismatic religious leadership is no less infused with politics. The devotees of religious charismatics are inspired not only by their message but also by their political skill and military success. In Jewish faith, for example, Moses is not just the prophet who brought the Law down from Mount Sinai: he is also the man of action who led the Israelites from Egypt to the Promised Land and, against the odds, molded this quarrelsome band of ex-slaves into a fighting nation. Isaiah is not just the prophet of moral virtue and the hope for universal peace at the end of days. He also guided Judah during the Assyrian invasion of 701 BCE, when he counseled King Hezekiah not to surrender (*Isaiah* ch. 39). Jesus did not only teach abstract universal principles of faith, justice, love and moral behaviour. By declaring that God is the only true king and that the eternal kingdom of heaven lies in the hearts of the faithful, he struck an indirect political blow at the temporal power of the Roman empire. Mohammed, too, did not only start a new religion: he was also a gifted military commander who conquered Arabia, unified its tribes under one faith with its centre in Mecca, and prepared the way for the expansion of the Islamic empire after his death in 632 CE.

The major religions of the ancient world were all official state religions. All exerted political power: Judaism in the kingdoms of Israel and Judah; Buddhism in the socio-political system in China and elsewhere in the Far East; Christianity in the Roman (Byzantine) empire; Zoroastrianism in the Persian (Sasanid) empire; and Islam in the empire created by Mohammed and his followers. The principles of faith in these religions were also political principles. These principles were almost invariably transmitted in a charismatic relationship. Many tenets of these faiths – for example, belief in one God, the war between good and evil, love of fellow men, submission to divine will, resurrection of the dead – could have been implanted and accepted among large masses of people in the absence of charismatic leadership. In theory, these ideas might be believed in and lived by because they are needed and life-enhancing, not because they are taught by extraordinary men. (The same is true of purely secular political or social movements in which a charismatic element is found, such as Marxism, Darwinism and Freudianism.) In practice, this is not the case. Each of the major religions, with the exception of Hinduism, has a single charismatic individual as its prime mover. Even Buddhism, which teaches the loss of individuality by merging with the universal life, has a charismatic as its central figure – Siddhartha Gautama, known as the Buddha.

The charismatic, whether in a religious or political group, typically has a sense of calling by destiny or by a higher being and a singleminded commitment to a cause. This calling is most likely to be recognized by a following in times of distress or crisis. His self-confidence and actions inspire his followers with confidence in his authority. They accept duty and sacrifice for him and the cause and this, in turn, consolidates the emotional bond, the union of leader and followers. Once the crisis has passed, his authority may continue in a more routine and bureaucratic form. These are visible similarities. There are also parallels in psychological make-up which are of equal, if not greater, importance: for example, the leader's familiarity with crisis and his ability to create, function and thrive in crisis; the interconnection between his inner world and external reality; and his idealistic vision of the future.

Many of the great political charismatics were born into families which were at least nominally religious, and were educated in religious schools. Some of their outstanding qualities are associated with religious leadership: Washington's personal humility, Robespierre's propensity for solitude and meditation, Garibaldi's asceticism, Lenin's fanatical faith in his movement. The violence used, to a greater or lesser extent, by these leaders in the name of their cause has many precedents in the histories of the great religious leaders and their followers. In politics as in religion, many charismatic leaders have persuaded large numbers of people of their supernatural or at least exceptional power, not because they hold high office but because of personal qualities. And although religious charisma by definition includes the supernatural, political charisma does not necessarily exclude the supernatural.

The longing for salvation – divine or demonic – in crisis may underlie charismatic leadership in religion as in politics. At times they even share a salvationist element in which crisis or distress is attributed to a deadly conspiracy the destruction of which would solve everything. A charismatic bond may thus be based upon resentment or hatred – for example of Jesuits, Freemasons, Communists, Capitalists or Jews – made all the more credible by the leader's earnest conviction and persuasiveness (Neumann, 1964).

Most unexpectedly, as suggested earlier, religious and political charisma are sometimes linked in having mystical or semi-mystical aims. These aims include the struggle to overcome alienation and the idealization of and union with a higher power. The drive for liberation, transcendence and union in religious charisma has close parallels in some political movements in which there is what John T. Marcus calls an 'empathetic identification with a hero-personality *seen as the transcendent self*' (1961, p. 238).

Finally, in politics as in religion, the leader's death need not mean the end of the movement. Still, the many failed religious leaders – the Dutchman Lourens van Voorthuizen, the Anglican priest Henry James Priest and the American Black preacher George Baker ('Father Divine') are some of the forgotten self-proclaimed messiahs of the past two centuries – are a reminder that religious charisma can be as fleeting as political charisma.

Even a limited comparison between religious and political charismatics brings out unexpected similarities. Mohammed and Robespierre, for example, may be compared in character, beliefs and aims. Both believed with fanatic passion in principles of faith and justice. They fought the socio-economic inequities of their times. They vigorously supported society's unfortunates, the widow and orphan. They were convinced that the rich have a social obligation to the poor and dispossessed. They believed in one God. They also shared certain similarities in background and psychological make-up. Both were inclined to an extreme, idealized, even brutal fervour in putting their beliefs into practice. Robespierre's identification with the widow and orphan, as we have seen, may be connected with his self-image as an orphan who lost his mother at age six and his father soon after. Mohammed's passion for social justice might be linked with a parallel trauma. According to Muslim tradition, he lost his father around the time of his birth and his mother by age six (Esposito, 1990, p. 8). These personal crises might have acted as a psychological schooling whose effects emerged in their rise to power in crisis later in life.

A similar comparison may be made between Moses and Paderewski, who in his day was looked on virtually as the Moses of Polish nationalism (Zamoyski, 1982). Jacob Talmon has observed a striking resemblance between Jewish and Polish nationalism. Both express the yearning of a people without a territorial homeland, 'a conquered, humiliated and oppressed nation dreaming of resurrection' (1967, p. 96). This comparison might be extended to charismatic manifestations of these nationalist movements. Here too, are hints of personal trauma finding an outlet in external reality. For Moses, according to the book of Exodus (2: 2–10), was separated from his mother soon after birth and raised by Pharaoh's daughter. The Bible implies a parallel between this personal separation and the exile of the Israelites from their homeland. Moses' charismatic bond with the Israelites was built upon his conviction of being divinely chosen to unite his people and lead them back to their motherland. His inner world corresponded with social reality to the point where he was driven to inspire the Israelites. They, in turn, instinctively saw him, despite his foreign background or because of it, as one who knew in his bones the torment of exile and alienation and the longing to return out of slavery to the Promised Land.

In certain limited ways, Moses' life and charismatic appeal are comparable with those of modern charismatics such as Paderewski. For in Paderewski's life, too, trauma might have affected, even determined, his public role. Paderewski was a 'Moses-figure' in having lost his mother a few months after birth and in being 'exiled' from his motherland. His semi-religious leadership of the scattered Polish people helped to inspire, unite and transform them into an articulate, influential lobby aiming at the restoration of Polish independence. He used his immense gifts and prestige as a concert pianist to this political aim. Yet, Paderewski was treated by his followers virtually as a divine being. His public appearances often had the naked awe of primitive religious ceremonies, through which he created a bond of love with his 'congregation' throughout the world (Zamoyski, pp. 4, 99, 103).

The many parallels between religious and political charisma mean that in practice the two are often indistinguishable. In the view of Norman Cohn (1972), the charismatic revolutionary movements of modern times had precursors in the millenarian movements among the rootless poor of Western Europe between the 11th and 16th centuries, e.g. the Taborites, the Adamites of Bohemia, the Ranters and the Brethren of the Free Spirit, who derived much inspiration and imagery from Judaeo-Christian eschatological writings. Cohn's conclusions support Weber's thesis that the most poor and ignorant on the social ladder are most radical in their need for a personal saviour:

> Amongst the surplus population living on the margin of society there was always a strong tendency to take as leader a layman, or maybe an apostate friar or monk, who imposed himself not simply as a holy man but as a prophet or even as a living god. On the strength of inspirations

or revelations for which he claimed divine origin this leader would decree for his followers a communal mission of vast dimensions and world-shaking importance. The conviction of having such a mission, of being divinely appointed to carry out a prodigious task, provided the disoriented and the frustrated with new bearings and new hope. It gave them not simply a place in the world but a unique and resplendent place. A fraternity of this kind felt itself an elite, set infinitely apart from and above ordinary mortals, sharing also in his miraculous powers. Moreover the mission which most attracted these masses from the neediest strata of the population was – naturally enough – a mission which was intended to culminate in a total transformation of society. In the eschatological phantasies which they had inherited from the distant past, the forgotten world of early Christianity, these people found a social myth most perfectly adapted to their needs (p. 60).

These millenarian movements were the background to the first great revolution in Western Europe, the overthrow of the English monarchy by Oliver Cromwell in the mid-seventeenth century. Cromwell's charismatic leadership was based in part upon messianic hopes, for in his time many Englishmen 'lived in daily expectation that through the violence of civil war the Kingdom of the Saints would be established on English soil and that Christ would descend to reign over it' (*ibid.*, p. 288).

Since the English Revolution, religious charisma has frequently affected secular Western nations. 'The French Revolution is a religion', wrote Condorcet in 1792, 'and Robespierre is one of its sects. He is a priest with his flock' (Matrat, 1975, p. 182). This view of the Revolution is overstated, but the perception of Robespierre is not. Robespierre came to regard himself, and to be regarded, not as a politician but virtually as the founder of a new religion. He aimed to reform the state through politics of morality. He learned this conception of government as a child at the school of St. Louis-le-Grand. Under the influence of his liberal atheist teachers, he stopped being a practicing Christian. He came under the spell of contemporary French philosophers, above all Rousseau, who taught that the state should be a school of moral rebirth. His dictatorial role in 1793–4 was consistent with the teaching of Rousseau. In *The Social Contract*, Rousseau argued that in crisis a state may need a dictator to save it. Robespierre believed in a God who protects the feeble and the oppressed, the widow and orphan. He was a fervent believer in an age of hostility to religion, especially in the revolutionary government. His beliefs derived partly from and were evidently compatible with his own inner needs and his self-perception as a once-helpless orphan. As an incorruptible defender of society's unfortunates, many of whom he had defended free of charge in his days as a lawyer in Arras, he came in the end to see himself as a messiah or a Moses-figure bringing the Law of Reason to the people. By the end of his life, he began to introduce these beliefs into French law. An example is the decree passed on 7th May 1794, the first article of which was that 'The French people recognize the existence of the Supreme Being and of the immortality of the soul' (*ibid.*, p. 253).

Robespierre's unusual living arrangements during the last three years of his life, from summer 1791, suggest rather poignantly the origins of his need for adoration bordering on idolatry, which was a vital part of his charismatic appeal. He had no family of his own but lived with the Duplay family, 'the image of a virtuous and united family, just as he hoped every French family to be. They might almost have stepped out of one of Rousseau's works' (*ibid.*, pp. 125–6). The children called him Bon Ami, and he treated them like an affectionate elder brother. In this home, he had a study full of pictures, drawings and engravings of his own image, a virtual Temple of the Self. Surrounded by four women, Robespierre seems to have enjoyed for the first time the love and care of which he had been deprived since age six, when his mother died. One visitor observed that in this sanctuary Robespierre received 'homage such as is only offered to a divinity' (*ibid.*, p. 127). This picture of Robespierre basking in the adoration of a devoted family seems strangely at odds with the image of the pathological tyrant, creator of the Reign of Terror, with its creed of the necessary murder.

Jacob Talmon (1952) has argued that a direct line exists between the political messianism of the Age of Enlightenment and 20th century totalitarianism. Liberty is incompatible with the idea of a logical, all-embracing, all-solving creed such as that of Robespierre:

> The two ideals correspond to the two instincts most deeply embedded in human nature, the yearning for salvation and the love of freedom. To attempt to satisfy both at the same time is bound to result, if not in unmitigated tyranny and serfdom, at least in the monumental hypocrisy and self-deception which are the concomitants of totalitarian democracy (1986, p. 253).

Nevertheless, empirical liberal democracy may benefit from milder forms of political salvationism, such as Roosevelt's in the 1930s. The most powerful images of traditional authority in Western culture in any case come from the Bible. This authority may be abused, as it was by Robespierre who, ever uncertain of his powers, tried to establish himself as heir to

Moses, descending the artificial mountain in the Champs de Mars at the Festival of the Supreme Being in June 1794.

The French took this symbolism lightly whereas the Americans at the same time were apparently much more serious in seeing George Washington as a new Moses. In his study of Washington, Barry Schwartz writes of biblical parallels as an integral part of Washington's charisma: 'As Americans became convinced more than ever that their country was the New Israel, the whole story of Washington's life was merged with that of the saviour of ancient Israel' (1987, p. 176). As leader of the Revolutionary army and later as first president of the United States, Washington underwent a virtual apotheosis as centre of a hero cult that verged at times on idolatry. He was seen as a symbol of faith, possessor of the attributes of God, executor of God's will; and he acknowledged the help of God in establishing the new republic and recommended religion as a secure foundation for public morals.

Not surprisingly then, charismatic political leaders are often linked – with various degrees of seriousness – with figures of religious authority, with priest and prophet, saviour and messiah, and at times with God. Robespierre in the summer of 1793, with France facing the crisis of invasion, 'was recognized as being the potential saviour of France' (Hibbert, 1980, p. 211). Similarly, the crisis in which Napoleon came to power in 1799 'was one in which Frenchmen in particular are ready to cry out for a saviour' (Butterfield, 1962, p. 37). Lincoln was 'the prophet and the man of faith' which America needed during the Civil War (Brogan, 1935, p. 49). And Robert Michels (1916) has shown that marked charismatic tendencies appeared in various West European socialist movements of the later nineteenth century, the leaders of which became objects of a 'cult of veneration among the masses' – Ferdinand Lasalle, for example, was received 'like a god' when he toured the Rhineland in 1864 (p. 70).

Garibaldi was self-consciously a messianic political leader. His beard and long hair gave him a Christ-like appearance. His behaviour was full of messianic symbolism. When he rode a white horse into Rome on 27th April 1849, he looked like 'a new Messiah' (Hibbert, 1965, p. 45). Later, in his campaigns in the Alps and southern Italy in 1859 and 1860, he was hailed virtually as the divine head of a new religion. Men kissed his feet, women thrust babies into his arms for him to bless or even baptize. His deeply mystical leanings gave the stamp of credibility to his religious authority. Like many spiritual saviours, Garibaldi despised orthodox religion. He hated priests and friars as traitorous scourges of Italy, the lying scum of humanity. And indeed, part of the trouble with Garibaldi, writes Christopher Hibbert, was that like Robespierre he took too seriously his messianic role. He lacked chiaroscuro in his vision, gripped as he was with fanatic certainty:

> There was sometimes a hint perhaps that his vision of himself as a man of destiny, the conscience of Italy, the prophet of a new religion, had impaired the simplicity and modesty of his character. He could never see how tasteless, how incongruous and how absurd were those lurid prints of him that depicted his Messianic features on the walls of so many poor homes – blessing the faithful, suffering on the cross, ascending to heaven, his vermilion shirt bulging against the azure sky. He never tired of reading about himself, of receiving idolatrous letters and enclosing in his reply a whisp of hair, a button, a piece of red thread. But then he could never see a joke, and that after all was part of his strength (*ibid.*, p. 364).

A prophetic or messianic streak similar to that of Garibaldi's is found among more recent political leaders in crisis. Herzl, for example, had a childhood dream in which the Messiah carried him to Moses, who said that he was the child for whom he prayed (Stewart, 1974, p. 282). Gandhi's influence, based not on a political organization but on sheer force of personality, was that of a religious leader: 'Gandhi showed that the spirit of Christ and of some Christian fathers, and of Buddha and of some Hebrew prophets and sages could be applied in modern times and to modern politics. He did not preach about God or religion; he was a living sermon' (Fischer, 1982, p. 461). Lenin spoke with 'the voice of inspired prophecy', and his arrival in Petrograd on Easter Monday 1917 heralded the 'resurrection' of Russia (Clark, 1988, pp. 200–1). Mussolini, too, was greeted by many of his followers as a semi-divine figure: ' "He is like a god," one of his *gerarchi* said as he watched him standing there with such Olympian passivity. "No, not *like* a god," his companion replied, "he *is* one." ' (Hibbert, 1962, p. 3). Churchill, similarly, is often described as a 'prophetic saviour' of Britain (Storr, in Taylor, ed., 1973, p. 245). Even Franklin D. Roosevelt, upon his inauguration as president of the United States in 1933, spoke to the nation virtually as a revivalist preacher and saviour. Frances Perkins, his labour secretary, recalled how like a great religious leader Roosevelt saw and understood his people in desperate need of spiritual purpose and direction; despair was the greatest sin, the enemy of hope, and Roosevelt was asking 'Do you believe?' as tears streamed down people's faces (Morgan, 1985, p. 374).

As for Hitler, it is not possible to understand the nature of his charismatic appeal without reference to religion. Up to a point the success of his revivalist style was attractive and admirable even to such an outspoken enemy of Nazism as Churchill (Manchester, 1983, p. 871). In the 1936 Nuremberg Rally, for example, Hitler spoke in the cadences of a messianic saviour:

> How deeply we feel once more in this hour the miracle that has brought us together! Once you heard the voice of a man, and it spoke to your hearts, it awakened you . . . you followed it, without even having seen the speaker; you only heard a voice and followed it. Now that we meet here, we are all filled with the wonder of this gathering. Not every one of you can see me and I do not see each one of you. But I feel you, and you feel me. It is faith in our nation that has made us little people great, that has made us poor people rich, that has made us wavering, fearful, timid people brave and confident; that has made us erring wanderers clear-sighted and has brought us together! (Stern, 1975, p. 90).

Citing this passage as an 'astonishing montage of biblical texts', J.P. Stern emphasizes that Hitler was reared in the Catholic tradition, which must partly take the blame for Hitler's crimes:

> [Hitler] was brought up in Catholic schools, liked to recall his boyhood impressions as a server at Mass and his early ambition to become an abbot. [Stalin's early ambition too was to become a priest.] He never publicly renounced his membership of the Church or ceased to pay his dues. He professed a cynical admiration for the Catholic hierarchy (not least after the Concordat of 1933), its world-wide organization, its educational policies and its pomp and circumstance . . . Above all he admired the Church's practice of recruiting her priests from all classes of society, and aimed at a similarly broad basis in the hierarchy of the Party. The anti-Semitic element in Austrian and Bavarian Catholicism provided him with a 'religious' legitimation of his own obsessive hatred of the Jews' (*ibid.*, p. 92).

Political charisma, even in democracies which separate church and state, retain many characteristics of traditional religious charisma. The background, inner life and psychology of the political charismatic are in some ways not unlike those of the great religious leader. In contrast with political charismatics, information about religious charismatics comes mostly from adherents. It offers few chances of balanced assessment. How many messiahs allow their biographies to be written, not by slavish followers and hagiographers but by a sophisticated unbeliever with full access to documentation and a free hand in the writing? There is one such messiah – Krishnamurti.

5 Krishnamurti: Reluctant Messiah

> 'I am like an India rubber toy, which a child plays with.
> It is the child that gives it life.'
>
> Krishnamurti

Jiddu Krishnamurti was 'discovered' as a Messiah in India when he was fourteen in 1909. For the next twenty years he was believed by tens of thousands of followers to be divine, revered and groomed by them to be the saviour of mankind. As the years passed, however, Krishnamurti became disenchanted with this role. In 1929 he publicly renounced it. He broke up the organization which had been created for him (the 'Order of the Star in the East') and launched out on his own as an independent religious teacher. Ironically, as a spiritual leader whose message was that one should not seek leaders but find the truth within oneself, Krishnamurti gained far more influence than he ever had as the Messiah. By the time of his death in 1986, he was one of the best-known and loved religious figures both in Western and Eastern countries.

Towards the end of his life, Krishnamurti allowed Mary Lutyens, a former disciple, to write his biography and gave her full access to his documents. Lutyens' work is unique among religious biographies as it is a documented work written by a non-believer, not in the spirit of hagiography but in order to depict as fully and truthfully as possible one of the most intriguing charismatic personalities in modern history. The result is the only critical authorized biography of a messianic figure, and Lutyens' biography therefore has a special importance in religious history.*

Krishnamurti's story began with the creation of the Theosophical Society in America in 1875. The moving spirit of the society was the notorious Russian, Madame Blavatsky, worshipped by her followers as a seer and miracle worker. The society set out, among other things, to create a so-called Universal Brotherhood of Humanity, without distinction of race, creed, sex, caste or colour. The breaking down of barriers between peoples was to be a dominant theme in Krishnamurti's teaching even after he

---

* Another important biography, by Jayakar (1986), though including some new material on the early years, is mainly about the period 1947–85.

45

broke with the theosophists. The society moved to India in 1882 and from there it rapidly became an international movement. Many of its early members were idealistic British Indiaphiles, notably the social reformer Annie Besant who converted to Hinduism, and included clergymen, artists and political leaders as well as a number of wealthy and well-connected, if somewhat eccentric aristocrats. By the turn of the century, the society numbered over ten thousand.

The central aim of the society since the time of Madame Blavatsky, who had died in 1891, was to prepare humanity for the Lord Maitreya, the World Teacher, who would bring a vital message in a time of dire need. According to the theosophists, the World Teacher had appeared in two previous incarnations: as Sri Krishna in the 4th century BCE, and as Jesus. In 1909, at the international headquarters of the society in Adyar near Madras, the third incarnation of the World Teacher was 'discovered' – Krishnamurti.

Krishnamurti was born in 1895, the son of Jiddu Narianiah, an Indian civil servant, and his wife Sanjeevamma. He was the eighth of eleven children, of whom six survived childhood. In 1905, when he was nine and a half, his mother died. This tragedy had a decisive impact on his inner life. Narianiah was hard pressed to raise his children, and his situation worsened when he retired two years later on half salary. As a longstanding member of the Theosophical Society, he appealed to its president, Annie Besant (who was looked upon in his house as saintly), for a job at Adyar which would provide accommodation for him and his family. His appeal was eventually answered. In early 1909 he moved with his children to Adyar where he worked as a secretarial assistant. The family lived in an overcrowded, dilapidated cottage without sanitation.

The boy who was to become the elegant Messiah was at this time marked with the effects of poor care. Undernourished, scrawny and dirty, his ribs showed through his skin and he had a persistent cough. His eyes were vacant, and he was thought to be dim-witted. At school he was often caned for his ignorance. He was sometimes compared with his mentally defective younger brother, Sadanand. He had suffered repeated bouts of malaria in childhood and was so weak that his father declared more than once that he was bound to die.

The 'discovery' of Krishnamurti was made later in 1909 by C.L. Leadbeater, a former English clergyman with a tainted reputation who for many years had worked closely with Annie Besant. Leadbeater was bathing in the Adyar river near the Theosophical Society estate when he saw among a crowd of boys a boy with 'the most wonderful aura he had ever seen . . . a most extraordinary aura' (Lutyens, 1975, I 21). (In later years,

Krishnamurti, who apparently had no memory of this momentous event in his life, would speak of 'the boy' as if he were another being belonging to some distant world and wonder in amazement why he had been picked out.) Later, after learning the boy's identity, Leadbeater resolved to train him as the human incarnation of the World Teacher. A believer in the transmigration of souls, he began to investigate Krishnamurti's past lives and 'reconstructed' thirty of these going back to 22,662 BCE. (In Hindu society today, and certainly at the turn of the century, such beliefs were by no means evidence of madness or even of crankiness.) He removed Krishnamurti (and his brother Nitya) from school and arranged private tuition for him while training him in spiritual leadership. In 1910 Krishnamurti's father was persuaded to transfer guardianship of his sons to Annie Besant. In 1911 the 'Order of the Star' was founded with the aim of preparing the world for Krishnamurti's messianic 'coming'.

These sudden, extraordinary changes seem not to have harmed Krishnamurti. One of his tutors, E.A. Wodehouse, brother of the writer, recalled his exceptional qualities:

> We were no blind devotees, prepared to see in him nothing but perfection. We were older people, educationalists, and with some experience of youth. Had there been a trace in him of conceit or affectation, or any posing as the 'holy child', or of priggish self-consciousness, we would undoubtedly have given an adverse verdict (*ibid.*, p. 45).

Despite the apparently responsible nature of the theosophists, Krishnamurti's father began to have serious doubts. In particular, he suspected that his son was being used in homosexual practices. He fought a long legal battle to regain custody, which he lost. By the end of the suit in 1914, Krishnamurti was settled in England, where he remained as a student until 1920. From then on, he travelled widely in Europe, Australia and the United States.

While in California in 1922, Krishnamurti was transformed by an overwhelming spiritual experience. For several consecutive days, amid excruciating pain in his head and spine, he had visions and hallucinations of the so-called higher Beings. He emerged from this trance-like state in ecstasy: 'The fountain of Truth has been revealed to me and the darkness has been dispersed. Love in all its glory has intoxicated my heart; my heart can never be closed. I have drunk at the fountain of Joy and eternal Beauty. I am God-intoxicated' (*ibid.*, pp. 159–60). The 'process', as Krishnamurti came to call it, continued with greater or lesser intensity for the rest of his life and is of paramount interest in any attempt to make sense of his charismatic appeal.

Krishnamurti's 'aura' was apparent already in childhood in the period after the death of his mother. Though he believed that one should live in the present and lose the memory of the past in the process of spiritual elevation, he did not diminish the impact on him of his mother's death. As a young man, his happiest memories were of himself and his mother together. Her death was a massive blow, all the more so as the conditions for mourning were poor. In a memoir written when he was eighteen, he recalled: 'My mother's death in 1905 deprived my brothers and myself of the one who loved and cared for us most, and my father was much too occupied to pay much attention to us ... there was really nobody to look after us' (*ibid.*, p. 5). Lady Emily Lutyens, his disciple and closest confidante during his years with the theosophists (and mother of his biographer), and whom he addressed as 'my holy mother', recalled his longing to be reunited with his dead mother. Her wish to compensate him for his loss illumines the mystery of his appeal, for no doubt many others responded to him, perhaps unconsciously, for similar reasons:

> His mother having died when he was very young, he was always yearning to be back in her arms. He had seen a picture in the *Daily Mirror* one day of a small boy seated on a bench in the Park and dreaming that he was sitting on his mother's lap. He cut out this picture and told me that he felt he was that little boy ... I longed to compensate him for his loss (*ibid.*, p. 82).

From an early age, Krishnamurti was inclined to 'spiritual' experiences owing to his unresolved grief. In common with many others who have illusions or hallucinations of the lost person, he had visions of his dead mother, which apparently signified his denial of her death and his yearning to be reunited with her. In Hindu society – and, in general, in the premodern world – such 'visions' were more likely to be regarded as evidence of contact with higher Beings than as signs of grief:

> I remember once following my mother's form as it went upstairs. I stretched out my hand and seemed to catch hold of her dress, but she vanished as soon as she reached the top of the stairs. Until a short time ago, I used to hear my mother following me as I went to school. I remember this particularly because I heard the sound of her bangles which Indian women wear on their wrists. At first I would look back half frightened, and I saw the vague form of her dress and part of her face. This happened almost always when I went out of the house (*ibid.*, p. 5).

Also, five of Krishnamurti's eleven siblings died in childhood or in early adult life. He was disturbed by these losses, and his sense of being 'chosen' and 'protected' by higher Beings might have derived in part from his having survived. In the year before his mother's death, he lost his eldest sister and discovered that he, like his mother, could occasionally 'see' the dead girl:

> I must confess I was very much afraid, because I had seen her dead and her body burnt. I generally rushed to my mother's side and she told me there was no reason to be afraid. I was the only member of my family, except my mother, to see these visions, though all believed in them (*ibid.*).

The impression of being dull-witted and vacant which Krishnamurti gave in his early years at Adyar, and which he later elevated into a spiritual virtue, was probably connected with his grief for his mother and his siblings as well as the difficult circumstances which followed these losses. In all probability, he was deeply depressed. His apathy and passivity at this time are poignantly illustrated in a story of him at school. The teacher asked him to stay after class but forgot to see him. Everyone went home except for Krishnamurti who remained seated in the classroom until discovered by a search party several hours later.

Krishnamurti's depression and his need for care may have called up Leadbeater's paternal or fraternal feelings – a younger brother of Leadbeater's had been murdered as a boy, and Krishnamurti would refer to Leadbeater as 'my eldest brother' (*ibid.*, p. 90). In addition, Annie Besant had been forced to part with her children after her divorce in 1873 (Nethercot, 1960, pp. 143–4). She never remarried or had other children. As much as Krishnamurti was attracted to her as a substitute for his lost mother – he would call her, too, 'my holy mother' (Lutyens, 1975, I 93) – she was drawn to him as a replacement for the children whom she had lost. Yet, although Leadbeater and Annie Besant 'discovered' and promoted Krishnamurti, the huge crowds which later flocked to hear him speak responded with similar rapture.

Krishnamurti's 'process', the immense unexplained physical pain leading to spiritual illumination and ecstasy, was also connected with childhood trauma. During the 'process' (for which he never sought medical treatment and which he claimed he could never afterwards remember), he would achieve his wish to return to his mother, 'to be back in her arms', as Lady Emily Lutyens put it. He would behave like a small child in need of its mother and would address the women around him as 'Amma' or 'Mother'. Mary Lutyens, was present on a number of these occasions in the 1920s and recalled that 'He had behaved to me at times as if I were his mother and he a child of about four' (1983, II 69n). Furthermore, she wrote: 'It seemed that only when he became a child again was he able to relax and thereby obtain some relief from the pain, which was with him all day now as a dull ache as well as intensely in the evenings. But he could not become a child without a 'mother' to look after the body.' (1975, I 184) At one point he had repeated visions of his dead mother, as he had in childhood:

> For the last five or six days I have been seeing my dead mother. Whenever I shut my eyes & especially during the evening when Rosalind [Williams, one of his followers], who looks after me during that period, is with me, I see her very clearly, in fact, I call to her aloud & mistake Rosalind for my long lost mother. It may be that she uses Rosalind or that R. is the reincarnation of my mother. I don't know which it is, nor is it of any importance. While I am in that state, I remember long-forgotten boyhood scenes, such as when I was ill with my mother, how I used to rest on her stomach!!, the beggars we used to feed & how I used to be waked up by her, & the going to school etc. (*ibid.*, pp. 165–6).

'It's strange,' mused Krishnamurti in his 1961 *Notebook*, 'how this process adjusts itself to circumstances' (1976, p. 31). There is little doubt that the pain, like his other ailments at various times – bronchitis, hay fever, digestive troubles and insomnia – was at least partly psychosomatic in origin. The pain would come on whenever he was quiet or alone with close friends, or if he were speaking about the past, his childhood in particular (Lutyens, II 229). It stopped as soon as he had to travel or meet strangers. His role as World Teacher, which obliged him constantly to travel and meet with strangers, provided him with a necessary diversion and respite from the pain. The circumstances in which the 'process' first began, in 1922, also suggest a psychosomatic cause. It began when he was alone, away from his family and from the theosophists, for the first time in his life. During the next two or three years, when it was most severe, Krishnamurti's two closest relatives, his father and his brother Nitya, died.

Krishnamurti's 'process' has parallels with the experiences of other mystics who suffered childhood loss, such as Sister Teresa, St. John of the Cross, Pascal and the Baal Shem Tov (Aberbach, 1989, 1993). As part of the 'process', Krishnamurti would have hallucinations of union not only with his mother but also with the entire world. The longing for union may be seen as the basis of his mystical-charismatic identity. Mystical experiences of belonging to the world, to a country, a higher ideal or Being, may be linked with unresolved grief and with charismatic appeal. In 1922, again, Krishnamurti had an hallucination which might be taken to foreshadow his later role as an international spiritual teacher. It shows how deep was his need and his impulse to identify himself with all animate and inanimate things:

> There was a man mending the road; that man was myself; the pickaxe he held was myself; the very stone which he was breaking up was a part of me; the tender blade of grass was my very being, and the tree beside the man was myself. I could almost feel and think like the roadmender, and I could feel the wind passing through the tree, and the little ant on the blade of grass I could feel. The birds, the dust, and the very noise were a part of me. Just then there was a car passing by at some distance; I was the driver, the engine, and the tyres; as the car went further away from me, I was going away from myself. I was in everything, or rather everything was in me, inanimate and animate, the mountains, the worm, and all breathing things (Lutyens, I 158).

Such hallucinations are not uncommon among the bereaved, who in normal grief may have temporary sensations of identification or union with with the lost person. In one study, a number of widows were conscious of coming to resemble their husbands or of 'containing' them. One widow described the following experience, which is not dissimilar from Krishnamurti's 'process': 'At dawn four days after my husband's death, something suddenly moved in on me – a presence almost pushed me out of bed – terribly overwhelming' (Parkes, 1986, p. 120). From then on, she had a strong sense of her husband's presence, either near or inside her. Another widow spoke of her happiness at having her late husband within her. Here, too, Krishnamurti's joy at being 'reunited' with his 'Beloved' comes to mind: 'It's not a sense of his presence. He's here inside me. That's why I'm happy all the time. It's as if two people are one' (*ibid.*, p. 121). As a transient phenomenon, the sense of union with the lost person is compatible with normal mourning. If persistent, it can become a pathological mechanism by which the bereaved attempts to communicate his denial of the loss and a disguised striving to recover the lost person (Bowlby, 1980, p. 289).

Krishnamurti's desire to 'belong to the world' might thus have been a direct result of his mother's death as he no longer belonged to a secure family. The need for reunion with his mother – a yearning 'to be back in her arms' – evolved into a need which could be satisfied – to be one with the Public, with the whole world and with the higher ideal or Beings, which he called his 'Beloved'. He eventually felt that he had attained unity with his 'Beloved', which he described as 'the open skies, the flowers, every human being' and which could be found 'in every animal, in every blade of grass, in every person that is suffering, in every individual' (Lutyens, I 250). In one of his most Christ-like pronouncements, he declared:

> I belong to all people, to all who really love, to all who are suffering. And if you would walk, you must walk with me. If you would understand you must look through my mind. If you would feel, you must look through my heart. And because I really love, I want you to love (*ibid.*, p. 233).

His break with the Theosophical Society in 1929 was accompanied by a new sense of union and self-overcoming. It is of great psychological interest that this spiritual turning point involved the conviction that 'henceforth there will be no separation':

> If I say, and I will say, that I am one with the Beloved, it is because I feel and know it. I have found what I longed for, I have become united, so that henceforth there will be no separation, because my thoughts, my desires, my longings – those of the individual self – have been destroyed . . . I have been united with my Beloved, and my Beloved and I will wander together the face of the earth (*ibid.*, p. 250).

Indeed, in a literal sense, Krishnamurti did belong to the world. He had no close family ties, never having married and having no children. He owned no property, had few possessions and no fixed home. Instead, he stayed in the homes of his followers throughout the world, and they were honoured to have him.

Why did Krishnamurti allow himself as a boy of fourteen to be taken up as a virtual deity? In later years he showed keen interest in questions such as these: 'Was he a freak? Why had he been picked out by Leadbeater on the beach?' (*ibid.*, II 170). His social and religious background was crucial. Like Sri Krishna, after whom he was named, he was the eighth child, and his mother was convinced that he would be in some way remarkable. He was steeped in religious rituals and beliefs, including the doctrine of reincarnation, and was familiar with many of the ideas and personalities of the Theosophical Society prior to his arrival at the society's estate in 1909. His 'visions' of his dead mother and sister, though part of his normal grief reactions, were taken as signs of supernatural power. In addition, there is the fact that after his mother's death his family was broken, impoverished and dependent on the Theosophical Society. He was also at a highly impressionable age when he came under Leadbeater's formidable influence.

Perhaps most important to him was his discovery of a new mother in the person of Annie Besant. Annie Besant was a woman of great character, charming and kind, and highly intelligent and sympathetic. She took Krishnamurti and his brother under her wing and let them sleep in her room as the conditions in their cottage were so poor. From Krishnamurti's first letter to her, it is touchingly clear that he loved her as a substitute for his dead mother: 'My dear Mother, Will you let me call you mother when I write to you? I have no other mother now to love, and I feel as if you were our mother because you have been so kind to us' (*ibid.*, I 31).

Inspired by his charismatic 'aura' and believing in their duty to prepare him for a world role, the theosophists worshipped Krishnamurti and gave him every educational advantage. Lacking self-esteem, he was vulnerable to such adulation, willing to 'belong to the world' as he no longer belonged to a secure family. His role as Messiah was a source of security, self-esteem and a diversion from 'things would hurt me more', as Lear says of the storm on the heath. There are worse careers. The theosophists became his family and within a year of his 'discovery', Annie Besant formally became his guardian. As in all charismatic relationships, both leader and followers needed one another: one to provide the 'gift', the other the conditions in which the gift could flourish.

Why did this relationship come to an end? Some of the reasons are fairly clear. As he grew older, Krishnamurti became increasingly mature and independent, and much as a son will break with his family and go his own way, he broke with the Theosophical Society at the relatively advanced age of thirty-four. Moreover, by the late 1920s, both Leadbeater and Annie Besant were spent forces, and the society depended largely on Krishnamurti who by this time was both intellectually and financially independent. (A follower had left him an annuity which was sufficient for him to live on.) He shrewdly recognized the right moment to get out. Perhaps there was also an element of psychological mimesis: as his mother had 'abandoned' him as a child by dying so also he 'abandoned' the organization which 'adopted' him. His dissolution of the 'Order of the Star' was a massive blow to thousands of his followers, including Annie Besant and Lady Emily Lutyens, who felt themselves to be spiritually bereaved. Despite his apparent passivity and dependence, there was a streak of anti-authoritarianism in Krishnamurti. Though he was taken in by the theosophists, he had no wish to be 'taken in' by their ideas and beliefs. Amusingly, he claimed never to have read theosophical literature as he found it boring and absurd. Mary Lutyens writes: 'When he was first "discovered" at Adyar it must have struck Leadbeater that the boy's empty mind was ideally fertile soil for the implanting of Theosophical ideas. So

it was, but what was not realized was that these ideas never took root'
(*ibid.*, p. 96).

Long before he broke with the theosophists, Krishnamurti privately
expressed deep misgivings about his divine role while continuing to play
it to the hilt. He described himself as a freak of nature (*lusus naturae*) and
as a 'crank of the superlative degree'; he asked 'Why did they ever pick
on me?' and expressed the desire to live a normal life as inconspicuously
as possible (*ibid.*, pp. 86, 111, 133, 139). His abhorrence of his messianic
role appears to have been strongest during the months before the 'process'
began in 1922. On his way to Australia to meet his disciples, he wrote to
Lady Emily what it felt like to be worshipped and subjected to ridicule by
non-believers:

> I am not one of these that longs for these kinds of things and yet it will
> be like this all my life. Oh! Lord, what have I done. Also I am so shy
> & ashamed of what these people will think, these fellow passengers,
> not that I care a damn but oh! how I dislike it all. Mother do tell me,
> what am I to do? I feel like a child, wanting to escape to its mother
> (*ibid.*, pp. 138–9).

A few days later, after his arrival in Perth, he wrote:

> You don't know how I abhor the whole thing, all the people coming to
> meet us, the meetings & the devotional stuff. It all goes against my
> nature & I am not fit for this job (p. 139).

And several weeks later:

> Heavens how I hate it all; it is not pleasant to have such notareity [*sic*].
> As I go about the street the people nudge each other & point me out;
> the other day one chap said to the other, 'There goes that chap printed
> in the papers, the Messiah!' Then they burst out laughing. I should have
> laughed too if I hadn't been there or involved in anyway [*sic*] (p. 145).

In the history of messianic movements, these touching confessions of
vulnerability and reluctance are probably unique.

Krishnamurti came to despise all organized religion, with its leader–follower
relationships – he once wrote that 'God is disorder' (*ibid.*, II 222) – and
he broke with Hinduism as he did with the Theosophical Society. Yet for
all that he hated being the Messiah of the theosophists, he apparently
never doubted that he was in touch with the supernatural: 'I really do
believe in the Masters', he wrote to Lady Emily in 1920 (*ibid.*, I 122). 'I

could feel the vibrations of the Lord Buddha', he wrote at the climax of his 'process' in August 1922:

> I beheld Lord Maitreya and Master K.H. [Kuthumi, a Tibetan religious teacher who had taken the Theosophical Society under his protection and who had instructed Krishnamurti]. I was so happy, calm and at peace. I could still see my body and I was hovering near it. There was such profound calmness both in the air and within myself, the calmness of the bottom of a deep unfathomable lake. Like the lake, I felt my physical body, with its mind and emotions, could be ruffled on the surface but nothing, nay nothing, could disturb the calmness of my soul. The Presence of the mighty Beings was with me for some time and then they were gone. I was supremely happy, for I had seen. Nothing could ever be the same (*ibid.*, p. 159).

Krishnamurti never lost his faith that he had, indeed, been chosen by the higher Beings, not for the Theosophical Society alone, but for all humanity. (He closely identified himself with Buddha, and it is interesting that he was once asked by his friend John Barrymore if he would portray Buddha in a motion picture, an offer which he turned down [*ibid.* I 237, II 48]). Throughout his life he would periodically feel the presence of these Beings, though only as a young man had he actually 'seen' them. When asked after the publication of the first volume of his biography in 1975 why, if the Masters existed, they had communed with him in his youth but not now, he replied: 'There is no need now that the Lord is here' (II 207).

Krishnamurti's genuine faith was an integral part of his charismatic appeal. After his highly impressive appearance before two thousand followers in Paris in 1921, Annie Besant wrote: 'the biggest thing about him was his intense conviction of the reality and omnipotence of the Hidden God in every man, and, to him, inevitable results of the presence of the divinity' (*ibid.*, I 129).

Another vital clue to Krishnamurti's religious psychology was his total vacancy of mind, his extreme absence of thought ever since he was a boy (though this did not stop him from writing over a dozen books). In 1979 he spoke of this vacancy to Mary Lutyens as a divine and profoundly mysterious gift:

> It would be simple if we said that the Lord Maitreya prepared this body and kept it vacant. That would be the simplest explanation but the simplest is suspect. Another explanation is that K.'s ego might have been in touch with the Lord Maitreya and the Buddha and said, 'I

withdraw: *that* is more important than my beastly self.' But I suspect this too. It implies a lot of superstition. The Lord Maitreya saw this body with the least ego, wanted to manifest through it and so it was kept uncontaminated (II 227).

Krishnamurti disliked psychological analysis and, while he believed in the higher Beings, he had no faith in Freud and the unconscious. His reluctance prior to Lutyens' biography to allow publication of the accounts of his 'process' was probably owing largely to the fact that this experience can be treated as a symptom of pathology rather than of spiritual elevation. Indeed, it is fascinating to see how his spiritual calling expressed and transcended his personal pathology. In common with many religious leaders in the past, he made spiritual virtues of qualities which could be interpreted as signs of childhood trauma and consequent inner disturbance: his sense of being 'chosen' and 'protected'; his almost total amnesia when it came to his early life; his vacancy of mind, aloofness and tendency to compartmentalize his friends and acquaintances; his weakness of ego; his abhorrence of sexual relationships as a source of contamination; and, most important of all, his 'process'. From a twentieth century perspective, it is astonishing that in his descriptions of the 'process' he does not once consider the possibility that the pain might not necessarily be a form of spiritual purification leading to illumination, but instead, of unconscious psychological conflict.

Practically all Krishnamurti's religious teachings have precedents in orthodox religion, yet many of these teachings bear the stamp of his own personal life, his psychological inclinations and needs. He found the 'Truth' within himself, and at the core of his teaching is that everyone can do the same. He was by nature passive and non-violent, a complete pacifist; this, he claimed, is an ideal for all humanity. He was deeply anti-authoritarian by nature; his teaching rejected leaders, spiritual as well as political. He was unintellectual – he failed university entrance examinations three times – and, for whatever reasons, he claimed to have practically no memory of the past; in his teaching he dismissed memory and knowledge as corrupting sources of prejudice, misunderstanding and conflict, and the past as a dead weight which one should try to obliterate. His life had been transformed in the instant in 1909 when Leadbeater spotted him on the beach at Adyar; again, at the heart of his teaching is the idea that every man can be transformed, can put an end to sorrow and find happiness – instantly. He had freed himself, first from his impoverished family, then from the strictures of the theosophists; 'My only concern', he said on dissolving the 'Order of the Star' in 1929, 'is to set man absolutely, unconditionally free' (*ibid.*, I 275). If his early family trauma had left him with a residue of inner conflict and violence, he sublimated his aggression by going to the opposite extreme of peace, harmony and the elimination of conflict.

Krishnamurti's charismatic appeal in all probability has the same basis as that of all great religious leaders: much as he represented an impersonal link with supernatural powers – or, at least, with the power to enrich one's inner life – he was delightfully human. He hated the routinization of religion, preferring golf, theatre, movies, music and poetry to religious ritual. Mary Lutyens, writing in the third person, recalled one incident in Sydney in 1925. Krishnamurti was briefly staying at The Manor, where Leadbeater now lived with a community of adherents:

All the young people at The Manor were sitting in a circle during a regular weekly meeting, with closed eyes, holding hands and meditating on their unity, when she suddenly opened her eyes to find K. grinning and winking at her through the window (*ibid.*, p. 205).

Krishnamurti had an infectious laugh – he loved P.G. Wodehouse and Stephen Leacock – and his close friends would occasionally see him laughing in tears at some silly joke. Though he was opposed to violence, he was a thriller addict and loved a good action film. Mary Lutyens went with him to see *Raid on Entebbe* in 1976: after the film, she recalled, he was shaking so much with excitement that he could hardly walk from the cinema. He was, surprisingly, an able mechanic and could dismantle clocks and cars and put them together again. He moved with seeming effortlessness from the sublime to the ridiculous, from communing with the higher Beings to telling ribald jokes or singing comic songs. His private life, though disciplined, was hardly austere. Though officially he had few possessions and he claimed that all he needed was quiet, he lived the life of a rich aristocrat, in fine homes and beautiful surroundings, he dressed well and was always impeccably groomed.

Krishnamurti's humanity lay as much in his helplessness as in his striving for omnipotence. While he claimed to be clairvoyant, he found to his chagrin that he could not control the ball at the gaming tables in Nice, though he said beforehand, 'it would be splendid if we controlled the ball by will-power and then we could bet as much as we liked & ruin the bank' (*ibid.*, p. 113). And although he claimed also to have the powers of a faith healer, he failed to save the life of his brother, Nitya. In 1924, the year before Nitya succumbed to tuberculosis, he had a dream which he related to Annie Besant in which he interceded with the higher Beings: 'I told him that I would sacrifice my happiness or anything that was required to let Nitya live, for I felt that this thing was decided. He listened to me & answered "He will be well."' (*ibid.*, p. 199).

Krishnamurti's child-like helplessness was apparent in his role as Messiah: such exceptional power is not needed by those who are content. He could not escape past powerlessness, the childhood losses and the distortions which followed. Yet, his example gives hope that creative power can spring from trauma. According to Krishnamurti, fear drives man to seek a higher Being or authority, whether human or divine. 'Destruction is essential', he wrote in his *Notebook*:

> Not of buildings and things but of all the psychological devices and defences, gods, beliefs, dependence on priests, experiences, knowledge and so on. Without destroying all these there cannot be creation. It's only in freedom that creation comes into being. Another cannot destroy these defences for you: you have to negate through your own self-knowing awareness (1976, p. 11).

At the heart of Krishnamurti's charismatic appeal is the belief in one's own inner power and the affirmation that trauma and inner violence can be transformed into a force for the good. In Krishnamurti's teachings, paradoxically, the refusal to worship a higher authority, whether divine or human, to project inner violence and distortion on to others, can lead to self-overcoming and freedom.

6 Paradoxes of a 'National Poet': The Strange Case of Bialik

'The rage of Dante against Florence, or Pistoia, or what not, the deep surge of Shakespeare's general cynicism and disillusionment are merely gigantic attempts to metamorphose private failures and disappointments. The great poet, in writing himself, writes his time.'

T.S. Eliot, 'Shakespeare and the Stoicism of Seneca'

The archetypal charismatic according to Weber is the biblical prophet, and so it is not entirely surprising that the renaissance of Hebrew language and literature as part of Jewish nationalism was led by a charismatic poet who, in some of his most powerful and influential works, spoke with the voice of a prophet – Chaim Nachman Bialik (1873–1934). One of the great, unexplained ironies of modern Jewish history is that Bialik, whom Weizmann called a giant of the Zionist movement, and who was hailed in his lifetime and until the present day as the poet laureate of the Jewish national renaissance, had painfully ambivalent feelings about this role – reminiscent of those of Krishnamurti, as shown in the previous chapter – to the point of rejecting it.

Instead, he saw himself in the humble role of an artist struggling with his personal agonies. Though he appeared in his poetry to be the virtual incarnation of a Biblical prophet (Maxim Gorky, who read him in Jabotinsky's Russian translations, called him a 'modern Isaiah'), he was emphatic in dismissing his public role, echoing the prophet Amos in the poem *Shaha nafshi* (My spirit is bowed, 1923): 'I am no prophet, no poet,/ But a chopper of wood.' His cynicism about writing of Zion is put frankly already at the start of his career: 'When you see me weeping for some wondrous land . . . do not mourn or comfort me, my tears are false' (*Dimah Ne'emanah* [Faithful Tear, 1894]). The motif of the poet tainted by the conviction of being a fake appears in some of Bialik's major poems, including *Davar* (The Word, 1904) and *Megillat ha-Esh* (The Scroll of Fire, 1905).

His friendship with Joseph Klausner, who later became professor of Hebrew Literature at the Hebrew University, was undermined by this

59

ambivalence. 'As a poet', Klausner wrote (1937), 'Bialik did not take certain nationalist–Zionist obligations as seriously as I thought was right and proper for him' (p. 114).

At the turn of the century, the growth of Hebrew literature was unavoidably bound up with the rise of Jewish nationalism, so that a Hebrew writer was generally expected to write about national themes. Though in a remarkably short time there would be an eruption of Hebrew talent, in the 1890s (when Bialik began to publish verse) really good Hebrew poetry was scarce. In fact, not long beforehand, Judah Leib Gordon, the best Hebrew poet of his generation, had lamented that he might be the last Hebrew poet. By becoming the first great poet in modern Hebrew, Bialik automatically became a cultural hero, with accompanying responsibilities. The guilt that these responsibilities brought upon him was exacerbated by his close relationship with Ahad Ha'am, the foremost philosopher of cultural Zionism, who exerted a dominant influence upon him, and whom he loved as a father. Ahad Ha'am, worried about the future of Zionism, called upon Hebrew writers to forgo free creativity and to harness their energies to the national cause. Whether Ahad Ha'am's influence stunted Bialik's creative growth is debatable; even before the philosopher moved from Odessa to London in 1908 Bialik's poetry became increasingly overt in its biographical content. His last poem, written shortly before his death, has not a trace of nationalism.

Bialik had no ambitions to become a national institution, but this is exactly what happened in his lifetime. He shunned the idea of being celebrated by the people, and suffered acute self-reproach over his status as national poet, feeling it to be undeserved. His first visit to Palestine, in 1909, started a wave of Bialik-mania; and to his disgust he was mobbed by crowds of enthusiasts who saw him as their prophet of revival. The Chief Rabbi of Palestine, Abraham Isaac Kook, set the tone for his reception, greeting him rapturously in the name of the people: 'Sing from now, O poet beloved unto us, of the salvation of a people and its God, waken your harp. Be filled with the power and beauty to sing for us a song of the land, a song of rebirth' (in Ungerfeld, 1974, p. 259).

To his wife, Bialik wrote from Jaffa, 'The people regard me as someone worthy of respect, but I know that I am a nobody' (1955, p. 40). The international fanfare which went on at the time of his 50th birthday weighed similarly on his conscience. He wrote at that time the poem referred to above, 'My spirit is bowed to the dust/Under the yoke of your love'; and he complained, with bitter humour, that he was used as a coin vulgarly jangling in the national coinbox. His view, expressed in work published posthumously (1971), of his poetry as illegitimate offspring, 'hybrid children of mixed seed . . . fruit of harlotry' (p. 148), might, among other things, reflect his guilt at writing personal poetry mistakenly thought to be national.

To all appearances, however, Bialik played the role of national poet to the hilt. His best poetry, written mostly in Odessa in the years 1900–11, was 'national' both in its enormous impact upon the Jews and, to some degree, in its intent. His poetic genius and rare knowledge of Hebrew sources, gained through his talmudic education, thrust him in the vanguard of Jewish writers who believed that if the nation was to be resurrected the language would have to be revived. He was adulated accordingly. The emotional climate which he helped to create was a windfall for political Zionism. Many Jews, raised to believe in the holiness of Israel and the Hebrew language, were as much under his spell as under that of Theodor Herzl.

Bialik wrote in an age of tragic social upheaval. The assassination of Tsar Alexander II in 1881 and the pogroms which followed were disastrous to the Russian Jews. The violence and discrimination against them together with their confinement in the Pale of Settlement and their severe economic restrictions drove them in vast numbers to escape – to America, to Palestine, or through revolution. With immense poetic energy, unmistakably reminiscent of the style and tone of the biblical prophets, Bialik seemed to convey not only the desperation which drove millions of Russian Jews to emigrate, but the burden of Jewish suffering in history:

> As our voices entreating lift into the darkness –
> Whose ear will turn?
> As our raw blasphemy streams to heaven –
> Over whose crown will it trickle?
> Grinding tooth, knuckling ire-veined fists –
> On whose scalp will the fury drift?
> All will fall windily
> Down the throat of chaos:
> No comfort remains, no helping hand, no way out –
> And heaven is dumb;
> murdering us with dispassionate eyes,
> Bearing its blame in blood-torn silence.
>
> *Davar* (The Word, 1904)

After the murderous Kishinev pogrom in 1903, Bialik was driven to write *Be-Ir ha-Haregah* ('The City of Slaughter'), the poem which cemented his reputation as national poet. He was barely 30 years old. No other modern Hebrew poem has stirred up such a public outcry in the

Jewish world. It is the only poem of Bialik's which, in the aftermath of the Holocaust, has the ring of prophecy. Yet for all its power to inspire national outrage, the poem is grotesquely dependent for its artistic success upon Bialik's uniquely personal stress. Moving like a funeral procession, the poem tells, at times with nauseating detail, of a journey into hell, revisiting the scenes of violence, the streets and yards stained with blood, the vandalised houses, the cellars where women were raped and their children murdered. The explosion of sarcasm and bitterness to which this leads at the end of the poem has for its target the cowardly, parasitical survivors who roused Bialik's ire for using this national tragedy to elicit sympathy and funds for themselves:

> Away, you beggars to the charnel-house!
> The bones of your father disinter!
> Cram them into your knapsacks, bear
> Them on your shoulders, and go forth
> To do your business with these precious wares
> At all the country fairs!
> (Tr. A.M. Klein, in Efros ed., 1965, p. 127)

Bialik's chastisement, while it makes for extraordinary poetry – and shook the Jewish people in a way they needed at the time – does not do justice to the historical facts. Bialik had been sent to Kishinev by Jews in Odessa to find out exacly what happened, and to write a report. He knew at first hand, therefore, that the pogrom was as severe as it was precisely because some Jews did take up arms and defend themselves; yet in the poem there is no mention of this. The opportunists who so infuriated Bialik were a minority, and their unheroic conduct did not warrant the emphasis which Bialik gives it.

An explanation of these distortions is that Bialik, perhaps unconsciously, identified himself with these *schnorrers* as he does elsewhere: his indignation with them for using naional tragedy for personal aims might partly have been a displaced form of self-chastisement for doing the same thing. In one of his early poems, *Hirhure Laila* (Night Meditations, 1894), God chooses him to be a *schnorrer*-prophet: 'Go round from door to door, knapsack on shoulder, go to the doors of generous men, bend down for a scrap of bread.'

Even in poetry which appears to express fierce nationalism, the mark of a troubled personality is found. Bialik's central achievement. *The Scroll of Fire*, begins with a spectacular account of the ruin of the Temple in Jerusalem, but abandons national catastrophe to confess the ruin of one man, apparently the poet himself, by the fire of passion.

The Hebrew reading public tended to overlook the idiosyncratic aspects of Bialik's art. The lopsided view of him was strengthened by his reputation as a charismatic political and cultural figure. He was one of the most influential Zionist leaders, frequently attending their congresses, and going on fund-raising missions. He was also an important man in Hebrew publishing, and in the field of Jewish education was looked upon as a pre-eminent authority. He co-edited the legends and folklore of the Talmud in the mammoth *Sefer ha-Aggadah* (Book of Legends, 1908–10), an achievement comparable in its way with what William Butler Yeats did for Irish folk literature and myths. Together with these activities, Bialik produced some of the loveliest children's poems in Hebrew, and over a hundred of his lyrics have been set to music. Bialik, in short, had a charismatic appeal to everyone, from distinguished philosophers to small children learning to read Hebrew, and to everyone he spoke in his own language. Few poets have had such success as spokesman of a nation, the representative of its cultural life and hopes.

To modern Israelis, Bialik is still the national poet *par excellence*, a classic who is highly praised and seldom read carefully. Amos Elon, in his book on *The Israelis* (1972), writes that 'None before Bialik nor after has expressed the Jewish will to live in words and rhymes of such beauty and poetic force; he is rightly known today as the national poet of Israel' (p. 162). Clichés such as these are typical of the literature on Bialik. They reflect the popular response to him as the servant of a cause rather than to the content of his work. Jewish nationalists naturally saw in his poetry what was most meaningful to them. The most influential of Bialik's 'national' poems, *The City of Slaughter*, is known to have inspired the formation of Jewish defence groups in East European towns; but the poem itself is pessimistic to the point of despair. Bialik's mature poetry has little of the 'will to live' for which he is commemorated in the traditional stereotype. Quite the opposite is true. In one of his morbid poems, *Lo herani Elohim* (God did not show me, 1911), the poet considers ways in which he might die, including suicide: 'perhaps through my very hunger and thirst for life and its beauty, with disgusted soul, braving the fury of the Creator, I will kick at his gift, and cast my life at his feet, like a defiled shoe torn from the foot.'

To his friend Ben Ami, Bialik wrote in 1907: 'Sometimes I feel like committing suicide – and I am too idle to do this good thing . . . What difference if I live?' (1937, II 46).

Bialik's art, like that of T.S. Eliot, was taken up by a movement which preferred to ignore – or remained ignorant of – the private, psychological reasons for writing, necessarily giving it instead a predominantly socio-political interpretation. Eliot's profession of the need for art to be impersonal did not stop him from disavowing the social import of *The Waste Land* which critics had read into it: 'To me it was only the relief of a personal and wholly insignificant grouse against life' (1971, p. 1).

And yet, it is not always undesirable to be misread. Bialik was fascinated, as Eliot was, by the subtleties of revelation, concealment, and deception in language – knowing, as Eliot put it in *The Use of Poetry and the Use of Criticism* (1933), that 'there may be personal causes which make it impossible for a poet to express himself in any but an obscure way' (1975, p. 150). In an essay, *Giluy ve-Khisuy be-Lashon* (Revelation and Concealment in Language, 1915), Bialik put forward the view that 'language in all its forms does not reveal its inner meaning . . . but serves as a partition, hiding it' (1958, p. 191). The persona of national poet was a convenient stay against over-inquisitiveness into his buried life. He writes in a late poem, *Gam be-hitaroto le-eynekhem* (Even when he wakes, 1931): 'Therefore he reveals himself, to be invisible and to deceive you. In vain you search the recesses of his verses – these too but cover his hidden thoughts.' While the excessive veneration for Bialik led him to feel misunderstood, and even perhaps restricted artistically, he might have been thankful at times to hide beneath the protective mantle of National Poet. A British psychiatrist, D.W. Winnicott, found the same dilemma in all artists: 'the urgent need to communicate and the still more urgent need not to be found. . . .' (1975, p. 185).

The disparity between Bialik's openness as a public man and the hidden burden of his private life – the mainspring of his art – was sensed by a few of his acquaintances. 'Bialik seemed always to be publicly revealed like a great open book,' wrote the poet Isaac Lamdan shortly after his death:

Few sensed that behind this openness gaped the depths upon whose banks the poet walked unseen. Few felt the hidden molten restlessness bubbling and fermenting deep inside this strong-seeming poet. Like foaming bubbles floating on the water which hint at a great tumult within, this restiveness showed in his physical nervousness, his speech, his facial distortions, his occasional heavy silences, the sudden depressed look on his face . . . Even when he was alive, we hardly knew anything about Bialik's hidden life. What do we know now? (in Orlan, ed., 1971, p. 370).

Bialik knew better than anyone that his emotional instability – and the art which issued from it – was largely a product of childhood trauma. Born in the Ukrainian town of Radi, Bialik was the son of a timber merchant whose business failed by the time the future poet was five years old. His mother, to whom he was strongly attached, was known for her wailing at funerals, a highly emotional and pious woman, troubled by the death of her first husband. The family moved to the nearby village of Zhitomir to start a new life, and the father set up as a tavern-owner (Bialik remembered him at this time studying *Mishna* while drunkards staggered in and out). Soon after, he fell ill and died, leaving three children. Bialik was about seven at the time.

Then occurred a blow comparable in its traumatic effect to Dickens' experience in the blacking factory. Bialik's distraught mother, having to go to work, was unable to care for him, so he was taken to live with his grandparents in an outlying suburb. Bialik was haunted by this memory to the end of his days, and although his mother was blameless, he could not help but feel betrayed. The death of his father and the forced separation from his mother – far more than the rise of Jewish nationalism – were the motivating forces and the focal points of his later life as an artist and a charismatic. Bialik's unease at being thought a 'national poet' can be attributed partly to his awareness of the importance of these personal factors in his creative life.

Bialik was never reconciled to his father's death, and continually felt the ill effects of having missed the benevolent yoke of fatherly discipline and motherly love. At the age of 50 (in a conversation with the Zionist leader Hayim Greenberg), he confessed that he thought of himself as 'an orphan who believes that a father does exist and that he might put in an appearance at any moment . . . this stems from weak nerves, from a certain ailment in the nervous system' (Greenberg, 1968, p. 307). Many years earlier he had written:

> If only my father had lived, if only I had grown on his knees . . . he would have educated me in his way, according to my abilities. He would have taught me: this is the way for you to go and I would not have been torn into ten pieces, my steps would have been sure on this chosen path. I would have had a settled mind, a man among men, knowing his worth, happy and successful all his days. But because my father died and I was raised by my grandfather, my education was passed into the hands of strangers and my defeat was entire (1937, I 3).

Bialik was in a life-long search for a father-substitute, such as Ahad Ha'am, and he projected his feeling of orphanhood on to his generation. In a commemoration of Ahad Ha'am in 1933, Bialik spoke emotionally of the absence of a strong leader (Weizmann, Ben-Gurion, and Jabotinsky were then in their prime): 'The generation which has no man to impose upon it his fearful authority – is an orphaned generation' (1935, II 210).

Bialik's life with his aged grandparents was restricted and puritanical, duty took the place of creative living, and inspiration was stifled. He was vulnerable to the onslaughts of relatives who had a notion of how to 'civilise' the boy. He remembered with especial disgust the torture of religious life which his grandfather imposed upon him, the endless learning equated with virtue, the *Talmud*, *Mishna*, Bible, the Zohar, the prayers each day,

> a hundred blessings, bundle after bundle of *mitzvot* [commandments], and the minutiae of *mitzvot*, and the minutiae of the minutiae from the day the Lord created the *Chumash* [Pentateuch] until the last book of laws or ethics was written down. . . . And all this labour the Jew is obliged to undertake, is forced to carry out, is not free to be rid of and escape from, even for one hour (1971, pp. 225–6).

This side-effect of his family's break-up was secondary to the great tragedy of his adult life – his childlessness – which cannot be ignored in attempts to understand his writing and the nature of his charismatic appeal. Whatever the reasons for his infertility (which his poetry constantly hints at), there is no doubt that he dearly wanted a child. The late curator of the Bialik Museum in Tel Aviv, Moshe Ungerfeld, who had known Bialik, once told me: 'You have no idea how much he wanted children. He was hungry for children . . .' In one conversation Bialik recalled a five-year-old girl who had travelled with him on a train (at that time there was talk of his being nominated for a Nobel Prize): 'I can't get this girl out of my thoughts . . . if that German woman were to give me little Else, I'd gladly renounce all the Nobel Prizes in this world and the hereafter in the next. Let Klausner proclaim someone else as the greatest Hebrew poet . . .' (Greenberg, 1968, pp. 300–1). Of the world from which Bialik came, Maurice Samuel has written: 'Childlessness was the great frustration . . . it was a dreadful thing for a Jew to die without leaving behind at least one son to say *Kaddish* for him at the appointed time' (1973, pp. 37, 39).

Bialik's orphanhood and separation from his mother are related in various prose fragments, and in the poems *Be-Yom Stav* (On An Autumn Day, 1897?), *Shirati* (My Poetry, 1900–1), and *Yatmut* (Orphanhood, 1928–33). 'My Poetry' purports to be a confession of the emotional sources of his poetry, particularly the period between his father's death and his removal to his grandfather's house. According to this poem his mother would labour in the market during the day and at home until midnight. At dawn she got up to bake bread: 'And my heart knows that her tears fell into the dough. In the morning, when she cut the warm bread, salty with tears, and I swallowed it, her sighs entered my bones . . .' Bialik never forgot the poverty of this period of his mother's degradation; he indicated that his endeavours for literary success were attempts to ensure that he would never know such poverty again. *Orphanhood*, Bialik's last poem, is the longest and most impasssioned account of this troubled period. Comparing himself in his suffering to the fathers of the three main religions, he emphasises the universality of his tragedy: he is not only Isaac on the verge of being sacrificed, but also Ishmael abandoned by his mother, and Christ crucified.

One of the likely effects of his orphanhood was the heightening of his response to the natural world, finding in it some of the attributes of parental love and care, and the paradisal emblem of the lost time before his father's death. There are startling similarities between his poetry of childhood and that of William Wordsworth, who also suffered orphanhood and the complete disruption of his family at the age of seven (and also passed into the care of grandparents with whom he was extremely unhappy). In his semi-biographical prose-poem, *Safiah* (Aftergrowth, 1903–23), Bialik writes of the language of nature, comparing it to the love which silently radiates from a mother to her child, constituting his bond with external reality:

> There was no speech and no words – only a vision. Such utterance as there was came without words or even sounds. It was a mystic utterance, especially created, from which all sound had evaporated, yet which still remained. Nor did I hear it with my ears, but it entered my soul through another medium. In the same way a mother's tenderness and loving gaze penetrate the soul of her baby, asleep in the cradle, when she stands over him anxious and excited – and he knows nothing (Tr. D. Patterson, 1973, p. 17).

The same idea is found in Wordsworth's *The Prelude*:

> . . . blest the Babe
> Nursed in his Mother's arms, who sinks to sleep
> Upon his Mother's breast; who, with his soul
> Drinks in the feelings of his Mother's eye! . . .
> Along his infant veins are interfused
> The gravitation and the filial bond
> Of Nature that connect him with the world.
> 234–7, 242–4, 1850 edn.

Separation from the mother or, in Wordsworth's case, her death, seems to have created in both poets the need for a mystic bond with the natural

world, a bond so strong that even inanimate objects would appear to have
the breath of life:

> There is a secret language of gods, without sound, only shades of col-
> our, made of magic, majestic pictures, hosts of visions. In this language
> God reveals himself to those he chooses, he meditates in it and uses it,
> creator that he is, to give body to his thoughts, to find the secret of the
> unformed dream. It is the language of images: a strip of blue sky and
> its expanse, the purity of small silver clouds and their dark mass, the
> tremor of golden wheat, the pride of the mighty cedar, the flap of the
> dove's white wing, the sweep of an eagle . . . the roar of a sea of flame,
> sunrise after sunset – in this language, tongue of tongues, the pool, too,
> formed me her eternal mystery.
>
> Ha-Brekha (The Pool, 1905)

This language of natural beauty through which God communicates with
his chosen ones is remarkably like that of the 'sense sublime' in Wordsworth's 'Tintern Abbey':

> And I have felt
> A presence that disturbs me with the joy
> Of elevated thoughts; a sense sublime
> Of something far more deeply interfused,
> Whose dwelling is the light of setting suns,
> And the round ocean and the living air,
> And the blue sky . . .

The bond with natural objects carried over from the bond with the
mother appears to have been an integral factor in the development of the
imagination. Bialik writes that as a child he was always imaginatively
'entering' objects such as trees or stones (Aberbach, 1981). In one such
anecdote in which he 'enters' the stove-mouth, a figure reminiscent of his
mother pulls him in (1971, pp. 237–8). Wordsworth's similar tendencies
to incorporate himself within natural objects and his self-confessed need
to convince himself of their reality might also be attributed in part to the
loss of his mother and the uncertainties aroused by this loss; for as he told
Isabella Fenwick,

> I was often unable to think of external things as having external exist-
> ence, and I communed with all that I saw as something not apart from,
> but inherent in, my own immaterial nature. Many times while going to
> school have I grasped at a wall or tree to recall myself from this abyss
> of idealism to the reality. At that time I was afraid of such processes (de
> Selincourt and Darbishire, eds, 1947, p. 463).

In writing of early childhood, though in a somewhat idealised way, both poets were engaged in a form of self-analysis, as if in creative response to the trauma of loss. The poetry of childhood might also have been an expression of a desire for children. After Wordsworth's first legitimate daughter was born, in 1803, he practically stopped writing about childhood; Bialik returned to this theme for the rest of his life. Most of the poetry which he wrote during his last quarter-century was for children, and he poured into this work the love which he wanted to give to children of his own: 'I will arise and go to the children, playing innocently by the gate. I will mix in their company, learn their talk and chatter – and become pure from their breath, wash my lips in their cleanliness' (*Halfa al panai* [Your spirit passed, 1916]). But his poetry for children was no escape, for Bialik could not suppress the themes of longing and deprivation which permeate his other poems. In some children's poems these themes are presented even more starkly:

> How shall I enter the gates
> Of the treasured land,
> If my key is broken,
> And the door is locked?
> *Me-Ahore ha-Sha'ar* (Behind the Gate, 1926–7)

Or, in another poem:

> In a corner, widower and orphan –
> A pale *lulav*, an *etrog* with cut stem.
> . . . My garden is ruined, its stalks crushed,
> Its ways untrodden.
> *Avim Hoshrim* (Clouds Darken, 1920s?)

The infertile landscape in Bialik's poetry, as in that of T.S. Eliot, might be the metaphoric landscape of his own infertility: the desert, the dry tree, the ruin, thunder without rain, melancholy in spring, the loss of hope and desire for death which accompany these images and others might reflect the emotional state of being childless. In one of Bialik's poems, the theme of 'April is the cruellest month' is particularly striking:

> Spring will sprout again, and I,
> Upon my bough I'll hang in grief –
> A sceptre bald, no flower his, nor blossom,
> No fruit, no leaf.
> *Tzanah lo zalzal* (A twig fell, 1911)

Elsewhere, too, the comparison with a dry tree is found: '. . . a root of dust, a withered flower . . . a single nest of thorns and thistles, an empty

shell, at my loins the staff of an oppressor – is this the tree of life?'
(*Gesisat Hole* [A Dying Man, 1893?]). Bialik's prose and poetry are filled
with imagery of this sort. The same imagery – the 'dead tree', the tree
'crookt and dry', the 'withered tree', the 'land of barren boughs', the
'hollow tree' – is found frequently in the works of T.S. Eliot. *Ash
Wednesday* contains the image of being cut off from fertility:

> . . . I know I shall not know
> The one veritable transitory power
> . . . I cannot drink
> There, where trees flower and springs flow. . .

Bialik's writings both illuminate and are illuminated by the works of
Eliot. Bialik's constant use of the landscape of ruin and waste land found
in Jewish legend and history – the destruction of the Temple (*The Scroll
of Fire*); the wanderings of the Israelites in the wilderness (*Aftergrowth*);
the impotent Israelite warriors stranded in the desert (*Mete Midbar* [The
Dead of the Wilderness, 1902); the quest beginning and ending by a ruin
to bring the Messiah (*Ha-Melekh David ba-Me'arah* [King David in his
Tomb]) – may have symbolic significance in the same way as Eliot's use
in *The Waste Land* of the story of the impotent Fisher King, the quest for
the Holy Grail, and the desert journey to Emmaus with the resurrected
Christ: these legends and stories might, on one level, point to the infertility
of the poet, and his desire for and failure to achieve sexual rebirth.

Most of the main elements in *The Waste Land* point to an anguished
obsession with infertility, and the entire poem revolves around the equa-
tion of fertile land with potency. The Fisher King, to take the most notorious
example, has suffered a sexual wound which has a homoeopathic effect on
the land, making it barren. Eliot's fascination with Greek drama – the
fragment 'Sweeney Agonistes' is a brilliant imitation of Aristophanes –
seems to have had a lot to do with the idea made popular by Cambridge
anthropologists such as Jessie Weston and Francis Cornford that the aim
of this drama was to promote fertility.

The underlying theme of childlessness breaks into the open only in
The Confidential Clerk, one of Eliot's late plays, written in the 1950s.
Although each of the older characters has had a child, every one is, in a
sense, childless. Two of them do not even know that they have children;
another has lost his son in battle; yet another has pretended not to be a
parent. At the beginning of the play, Sir Claude Mulhammer explains to
his retiring clerk, Eggerson, that his new clerk, Colby Simpkins, is to be
introduced to his wife, Lady Elizabeth, as 'Mr Simpkins', not as 'Colby':

Sir Claude:	The reason for meeting him as merely Mr. Simpkins,
	Is, that she has a strong maternal instinct . . .
Eggerson:	I realise that.
Sir Claude:	Which has always been thwarted.
Eggerson:	I'm sure its been a grief to both of you
	That you've never had children.

His childlessness has induced in Sir Claude an overwhelming feeling of having failed in life, despite his worldly success. He would have liked to be a potter, and his yearning to create 'life itself' out of china or porcelain transparently reveals a desire for children:

> . . . nothing *I* ever made ever gave me that contentment –
> That state of utter exhaustion and peace
> Which comes in dying to give something life . . .

Valerie Eliot, the poet's second wife, has told me that her husband was a naturally paternal man who should have had a large family. In spite of his phenomenal achievement and fame, he was afflicted at the end of his life by a strong sense of failure and disappointment. Precisely the same things have been said about Bialik, with the explanation that his childlessness caused him a massive feeling of inferiority. This attitude is evident in the mood of negation in the writings of both poets. The words 'not' or 'nothing' are frequent. Bialik, for example, writes that he is 'nothing, a nobody', he is 'no prophet, no poet', 'I have nothing but a frightened soul': and Eliot turns away from ordinary life, 'I cannot hope to turn again', to the belief that one must 'go by a way wherein there is no ecstasy.'

Bialik and Eliot are part of a long literary tradition of using vegetable infertility to symbolize childlessness. The childless man and the dry tree are linked in the Biblical verse, 'Neither let the eunuch say: "Behold I am a dry tree"' (*Isaiah* lvi 3). Macbeth uses similar imagery in speaking of his childlessness: 'Upon my head they placed a fruitless crown.' D.H. Lawrence, in *Lady Chatterley's Lover*, has the impotent Clifford Chatterley confess the torment of his childlessness in a ruined wood, with 'long sawn stumps showing their tops and their grasping roots, lifeless.' He says: 'I mind more, not having a son, when I come here, than any other time' (ch. 5).

Predicate thinking of this sort is found in Bialik's extraordinary sensitivity to images of ruin and infertility, a characteristic which struck the poet Jacob Fichman: 'Each time that he saw the slightest sign of ruin in the fence or a dry branch on a tree he was extremely troubled by the

sight . . .' (1946, p. 368). He wrote the poem 'A twig fell' after seeing a
broken branch:

> Like the twig that falls across the gate,
> Sleep comes to me:
> My fruit has fallen, what helps me now
> My branch or tree?

One source of Eliot's creative impulse was a similar vulnerability to
images like these. When he visited Burnt Norton in the 1930s and later
wrote a poem with that title, he seems to have been moved specifically by
the dry pool, the empty house, and the children playing in the garden –
'What might have been and what has been' – as objective correlatives of
his childlessness. Imagery such as this, expressed with great pessimistic
authority, could be (and often was) taken to reflect the barrenness and
impotence of a society, urgently in need of change.

An analysis of the themes of bereavement and infertility in Bialik's
writings, while making clearer his significance as a deeply personal artist of universal interest, provides extraordinary insight into his role as
national poet. His charismatic appeal can be attributed to this side of his
work, which seems, on the surface, to have the least to do with nationalism. The great blows to Jewish nationhood have traditionally been expressed
in imagery of bereavement and in a tone of loss remarkably like that in
Bialik's poetry. Bialik's longing for his childhood and for his mother (who
while still alive was, nevertheless, out of reach) seems to have corresponded with the national longing for Zion, for the imaginary lost paradise
of the nation's childhood, for a land which, like the mother, still existed,
but seemed equally beyond reach. Partly for this reason, he spoke to his
'orphaned generation' with particular conviction.

The personal equivalent of the loss of the national homeland is bereavement, for a bereaved person, especially an orphan deprived of a secure
home, knows most intimately the resulting confusions, the instability, and
the terrors. Already in the Book of *Ezekiel* (ch. 24) the tragedy of the
individual and of the nation are symbolic of each other: the death of the
prophet's wife both represents and is represented by the destruction of
the Temple and the fall of Judah. Not surprisingly, the greatest Hebrew
poet of Zion before Bialik, Judah Halevi, is also believed to have suffered bereavement in early childhood.

The imagery of infertility is also found in traditional depictions of
national calamity. In the Bible, the fall of the kingdoms of Israel and
Judah is depicted in images of barren fields and vineyards, rotten fruit,
leaves and roots. In the Book of *Ezekiel*, the fall of Judah is related both in

imagery of infertility and bereavement: 'Your mother was like a vine in a vineyard transplanted by the water . . . But the vine was plucked up in fury, cast down to the ground; the east wind dried it up; its fruit was stripped off, its strong stem was withered; the fire consumed it' (19:10, 12–13, RSV). Bialik chastens the people, using the same epithets with which he chastises himself: they are dry as a tree, withered like grass, immobile, useless, rotten from head to foot.

One of the persistent themes in Jewish liturgy is the yearning to renew the days gone by, a motif prominent in Bialik's poetry of childhood. The hope for national renewal for 'a new heart and a new spirit', dates from the time of the exile of the Israelite nation by the Babylonians – when it became politically impotent and spiritually an orphan. Bialik occasionally, though not frequently, identified the nation's hopes as his own:

> My might is that of the nation!
> I too have power enough!
> In open spaces set free my imprisoned strength!
> A weak nation will blossom,
> My rotten bones will flower like grass.
> *Iggeret Ketanah* (A Short Letter, 1894)

Elsewhere, the poet imagines himself cutting out his heart and hammering it, filling it with new strength. For the most part, a halo of sadness and pain hovers over Bialik's work. The hope for the renewal of the self – as of the nation – is defeated.

More clearly than most poets, Bialik bears out Lionel Trilling's contention that 'the elements of art are not limited to the world of art . . . anything we may learn about the artist himself may be enriching and legitimate' (1970, p. 61). Bialik is the principal subject of his poetry, a Romantic tormented by what he had lost in life and could never regain. In life-long mourning for his childhood, he spoke meaningfully to a people in perpetual mourning for its lost nationhood. The elegaic tone of his poetry is that of the Jewish people in exile. Bialik's private agony mirrored national trauma in such an extraordinary way that the two became intertwined and inextricably linked in the poetry.

7 Charisma and the Media

The modern media, epecially film and radio, have enormously expanded the possibilities and the meaning of charisma. No sooner is a medium invented than it is used as a vehicle for charisma. The invention of cinema opened the way to Charlie Chaplin, whose film career began in 1914, shortly after the first feature film was made. By the late 1920s, radio and the newsreel coupled with commercial air travel – all newly-developed – were used with diabolical effectiveness by Hitler in his electoral campaigns (Kershaw, 1987). By the 1960s, television became a tool of charismatic, or semi-charismatic leaders such as John F. Kennedy and Charles de Gaulle.

In some ways, the idea of charisma has been trivialized in a world shrunk by technology into a so-called 'global village' in which large numbers of people can become instantly famous. Pseudocharisma is often stimulated artificially, through the use of propaganda techniques and opinion polls, to create the illusion of charismatic leadership (Bensman and Givant, 1975). In journalism, the word 'charisma' or 'charismatic' is nothing more than a catchword, interchangable with 'popular' or 'attractive'. It describes film stars, singers, politicians, men and women in business or sports, most of whom vanish without a trace.

The life and career of T.E. Lawrence ('Lawrence of Arabia'), one of the few modern charismatics whose appeal has proven to be enduring, illustrates the susceptibility of film in its infancy to abuse through the manufacture and manipulation of charisma. For Lawrence's image was at variance with the accomplishments, the character and self-image of the real person, but was accepted by an unsophisticated, charisma-hungry audience. Especially in the silent films and the accompanying lectures and written accounts of Lowell Thomas which attracted audiences in the millions after World War I, Lawrence's image was simplified as the clean, romantic hero, a swashbuckling Englishman in Arab dress leading the Arab Revolt to a glorious victory over the tyrannical Turks, allies of the hated Hun.

This image satisfied a hunger for heroism and romance and, as Lawrence's authorized biographer, Jeremy Wilson (1989), writes, it 'provided audiences with a welcome relief from the horrors of the Western Front' (p. 626). Yet part of the fascination of Lawrence is that he despised his charismatic persona while genuinely longing for heroism; and, as Wilson shows, he confessed in letters and diaries a painful awareness of the conflict between the media image and the reality. Lawrence emerges in his own writings as a sensitive artist and scholar who, though a brilliant military commander, loathed war. The main trauma of his adult life – his homosexual rape as a prisoner at the hands of the Turks in 1918 – tormented him with guilt, rage and self-disgust for the rest of his life. But even as a child he was inclined to feelings of inferiority and insecurity which, to a large extent, determined his character. His illegitimate birth was a cause of great bitterness, driving him to attain dramatic success and fame as a means of establishing securely and beyond doubt his social position. Self-conscious over his short stature, he was impelled further to large ambition. Above all, his mother's domineering character ensured that he would remain a solitary figure, unable to lose himself in love and in normal family life, and therefore able to devote all his considerable intelligence and energy to his career.

The pure heroic figure of film and the press derived from this strange, complex-ridden, private man. Fearless in battle, Lawrence was afraid of women, of sex and of family life and engaged in self-flagellation, physical as well as psychological. He linked his revulsion at the opposite sex to his mother's actual or perceived attempts to dominate and meddle in his private life, which in his adolescence drove him to escape home and join the army. 'I have a terror of her knowing anything about my feelings, or convictions, or way of life,' he wrote of his mother to Charlotte Shaw. 'She has given me a terror of families ... Knowledge of her will prevent my ever making any woman a mother, and the cause of children' (p. 32).

His recoil against maternal intrusion (which was mimicked in his later aversion to a persistently meddling media) inclined Lawrence to seek what were then male-dominated professions – first archaeology, then the civil service, the army and the RAF, as well as his solitary work as a writer – which cut him off from women. The Revolt was a male domain. (It may be psychologically significant, too, that in the Arab society in which he thrived, the family structure was the reverse of his own: the male was dominant.) The war, too, produced in Lawrence recurrent symptoms of post-traumatic stress disorders, for which he never received professional help and which further inhibited his capacity for affectional bonds. He confessed to Lady Astor his incapability of close relationships, for his heart was a 'monstrous piece of machinery ... till now it has never cared for anyone' (p. 913); and as for his work at the RAF, he wrote, 'Being a mechanic cuts one off from all real communication with women' (p. 923). The film of 'Lawrence of Arabia' presents the desert in all its magnificent barrenness virtually as an emblem of this waste land of the heart. Prone to depression, Lawrence diverted himself from emotional stagnation through literature and music as well as through action and motion: he was a connoisseur of planes, speedboats and motorcycles in their infancy, and was killed speeding.

Just as Lawrence was aware that his character was grossly misrepresented, so also he acknowledged privately and, later, in the various drafts of his memoir of the Arab Revolt, *The Seven Pillars of Wisdom* (1926), that his own motives were distorted by the media. A paradox of Lawrence's charisma was that he was inspired by the conviction that the Arabs should be granted independence but acted as an agent of British imperialism. He was ashamed of the assurances which he gave them that they were fighting for independence. If there was a single ideal which ruled him, it was freedom, both personal and national. In this respect, Lawrence was not unlike Kennedy, as we have seen in Chapter 1. In his dedication to *The Seven Pillars of Wisdom*, he expresses the poetic ideal underlying his commitment to the Arab cause:

> I loved you, so I drew these tides of men
>> into my hands and wrote
>> my will across the sky in stars
>
> To earn you Freedom, the seven-pillared
>> worthy house, that your eyes
>> might be shining for me
>
> When we came.

At the time of the Revolt, he confessed his hypocrisy, describing himself and his actions in terms which undermine the media image, as 'dishonest', 'immoral', 'sordid' and 'false': he was 'almost the chief crook of our gang' (p. 414). As in the case of Bialik and Krishnamurti, he hated his public role: 'Had I been an honest adviser of the Arabs I would have advised them to go home and not risk their lives fighting for such stuff ... We are calling them to fight for us on a lie, and I can't stand it' (p. 410).

Nevertheless, Lawrence was not merely created and used by the media but in some ways created his own public image. Through his charismatic role, he harnessed qualities of character which in normal life made him a misfit, to a corresponding political reality in which he was crucially important. These qualities included a remarkable combination of nobility, chivalry, bravery and high intelligence, integrity, asceticism and self-control. Lawrence struggled to bypass the disability imposed upon him by his aversion to women and to overcome the inferiority and insecurity of being illegitimate. It is striking how Lawrence's own sense of inferiority and of fallen aristocracy corresponded with that of the Arabs whom he led, who felt themselves to be heirs of a great civilization but were in a position of military and political subjugation to the great imperial powers. Emotionally imprisoned, Lawrence empathized with nationalist yearnings of oppressed peoples – he approved of Zionism as well as Arab nationalism – and with their struggle for freedom. So enthusiastic was he to justify and make legitimate Arab independence that in *The Seven Pillars of Wisdom* he glosses over the failings and weaknesses of the Arab Revolt, as well as the enormous contribution made by non-Arab personnel, including the RAF whose bombing and reconnaissance had been decisive in the northern campaign (p. 630). The Revolt added speed and lustre to the campaign, but Lawrence does not make clear that militarily it was largely superfluous.

After the Paris Peace Conference of 1919, Lawrence withdrew from Middle Eastern affairs and left government service. He never revisited the scenes of his triumphs. Instead, he embarked on a quest for self-discovery, self-realization and obscurity as a writer and as an enlisted man under an assumed name. Yet his enlistment continued a pattern to which his leadership of the Arabs also belonged: it brought him social relationships and situations which assuaged his feelings of inferiority and illegitimacy. In the ranks, Wilson points out (p. 670), Lawrence's intellectual superiority was effortless and unrivalled. Lawrence gravitated to roles that were subservient and self-abasing while at the same time gratifying strong ambition. (Nothing could have been more calculated to stir up media hunger than his efforts to ensure obscurity in the army and the RAF.) His letters to Charlotte Shaw reveal the paradox of his sense of inferiority co-existing with a conviction of being a power behind the throne: 'I long for people to look down upon me and despise me' (p. 766); 'Feisal owed me Damascus first of all, and Bagdad [*sic*] second; and between those stages most of his education in kingcraft and affairs. When with him I am an omnipotent adviser . . .' (p. 806).

The truth of Lawrence's motives both contradicted and made possible his media image. A strong base for the charismatic bond between Lawrence and his audience was a lapsed faith reawakened in secular form by a need to seek meaning in 'the war to end all wars.' Lawrence's parents were staunch Protestants. Lawrence received a strongly religious upbringing and was unusually receptive to religious instruction (pp. 26–7). As Arab manqué, he personified a return to a primitive, biblical world of faith in a modern crusade to conquer the Holy Land and rid it of the infidel, this time backed up by science, by armour, guns and planes.

Science has created media which have in some ways watered down the traditional religious force of charisma. Yet, as in the case of Lawrence, it has also magnified as never before the public view of charismatics. It has uncovered much that was previously hidden about charisma in its traditional forms and enhanced the possibilities for charismatic religious expression in popular culture. Charles Lindbergh, for example, became a symbol of semi-religious charismatic authority when he made the first non-stop flight across the Atlantic in 1927: 'When he returned to earth,' writes Leo Braudy (1986), 'crowds pressed into his aura to receive the benediction of his presence as if he were some kind of secular priest' (p. 21).

In at least one case, that of Albert Einstein, the scientist has become a semi-religious icon of popular culture. Einstein's international fame dates from 1919. In that year, a part of his General Theory of Relativity – the deflection of starlight in the gravitational field of the sun – was proved during an eclipse. This discovery established Einstein virtually as a modern Moses. He spoke the sacred language of mathematics, communed with the higher powers and returned to man with new laws, a different picture of the universe and a fresh self-perception. All this was life-giving after the slaughter of the Great War. Einstein himself indirectly encouraged this view of his charismatic appeal. He made no secret of the fact that he regarded mystical sensation as the origin of all true science. He retained a lifelong child-like awe at the presence of an impenetrable higher power, infinitely wise and beautiful. His colleague, the physicist Abraham Pais, described the religious character of Einstein's mass appeal:

The essence of Einstein's unique position . . . has everything to do, it seems to me, with the stars and with language. A new man appears abruptly, the 'suddenly famous Doctor Einstein.' He carries the message of a new order in the universe. He is a new Moses come down from the mountain to bring the law and a new Joshua controlling the motion of heavenly bodies. He speaks in strange tongues but wise men aver that the stars testify to his veracity. Through the ages, child and adult alike had looked with wonder at stars and light. Speak of such new things as X-rays or atoms and man may be awed. But stars had forever been in his dreams and his myths. Their recurrence manifested an order beyond human control. Irregularities in the skies – comets, eclipses – were omens, mainly of evil. Behold, a new man appears. His mathematical language is sacred yet amenable to transcription into the profane: the fourth dimension, stars are not where they seemed to be but nobody need worry, light has weight, space is warped. He fulfils two profound needs in man, the need to know and the need not to know but to believe. The drama of his emergence is enhanced . . . by the coincidence – itself caused largely by the vagaries of war – between the meeting of the joint societies and the first annual remembrance of horrid events of the recent past which had caused millions to die, empires to fall, the future to be uncertain. The new man who appears at that time represents order and power. He becomes the θεῖος ἀνήρ, the divine man, of the twentieth century (1982, p. 311).

Though scientists created the modern media, Einstein is exceptional as a scientific charismatic. The charismatic uses of the media have fallen mostly to politicians and entertainers. Whereas religious and political charismatics often create a public persona into which they disappear, the most serious entertainer-charismatics set out to explore their inner world and, indirectly, the sources of their appeal. As in politics, entertainment retains more than a veneer of religion. The language of religion is used to describe charismatics such as Sarah Bernhardt or Marilyn Monroe. They are 'worshipped' by their 'devotees' who are 'enchanted' by their 'spell' as by a 'goddess' (e.g. Brandon, 1991; Summers, 1985). The career of Paderewski was a heady brew of hype, art, politics and genuine religious feeling. The pianist exerted hypnotic power over his audiences, arousing a mass delirium (known in its day as 'Paddymania') characteristic of the effect of Chaplin or the Beatles later on. A large industry grew around his image, in the form of wigs, toys, candles, mechanical toys, even soap and shampoo. His impact as a pianist and a political leader was not unlike that of a great religious leader. His performances were, as seen previously, less music or politics than religious ceremony. His greatest achievement – the unification of the Polish community and its transformation into an articulate lobby for Polish independence – was virtually that of a religious leader rather than that of a politician for, as Zamoyski (1982) writes, he created a 'bond of love between him and a congregation which came to embrace millions throughout the world' (p. 4). His audiences '*willed* to see him as the transcendent artist, they willed to see him beautiful, magnificent, almost divine' (p. 99). In the ambiguous identity which he created of being mass entertainer and religious leader, Paderewski anticipated many popular artists, especially those whose art had its origins in religion – the soul and spiritual singers, the ragtime players, the gospel, blues and rock singers.

'The World's Greatest Entertainer', as Al Jolson was billed between the wars and after, was rooted in Jewish religious culture, though he was largely alienated from it and assimilated into secular American show business society. Jolson in live performance, Herbert G. Goldman (1988) writes in a profusion of inadequate adjectives, was electric, magnetic, galvanic, captivating, thrilling: 'Jolson's stage persona was like God's (p. 76). The Russian-born son of a combination rabbi–cantor–Jewish religion teacher, Jolson brought to the stage much of the soul of the cantorial tradition, its joyous creative energy and optimism, its melancholy beauty and pathos. His best-known role, in *The Jazz Singer* (1927), the first talking picture, was written with him in mind: the cantor's son who is torn between loyalty to his religion and family and the enticing world of popular entertainment (Gabler, 1988, p. 141). The film ends with a compromise of sorts, first with Jolson taking his ailing father's place as cantor on Yom Kippur, then in a theatre in blackface singing 'Mammy'.

'Mammy' was probably Jolson's greatest song, the one which meant most to him and which went deepest into his psychology and the sources of his charismatic appeal. For Jolson's life as a performer was inseparably linked, Goldman writes, with the death of his mother when he was eight:

> In many senses, Jolson would sit *shiva* [the seven days of Jewish mourning] for his mother all his life. And because his mourning was never completed, he continually experienced deep loneliness. When Naomi [his mother] died, he thought that his own life had ended. He needed love but it was not forthcoming. From now on, he felt, the love his mother had given him would have to come from somewhere else – from outside of the family . . . (p. 14).

His withdrawal after her death was arrested by a visit to the theatre a few months later: 'At the age of nine, he had found a new life in the theatre, and a new source of love in the sound of applause. All previous memories were submerged, buried. From now on, he had but one goal – to perform' (p. 15).

More blatantly than Jolson, Elvis Presley was treated – and regarded himself – as divine. Convinced that his gift was God-given, he saw himself as a latter-day Jesus, a messianic crusader for spiritual enlightenment and moral rebirth, hypocrite though he was in his addictions. He claimed to have visions, to hear voices, to work miracles. He immersed himself in spiritualist tracts – Madame Blavatsky, Richard Maurice Bucke, Annie Besant and Krishnamurti. Identified at first, in the 1950s, with delinquency and licentiousness, Presley was in fact a gospel singer of rare lyric tenderness, and his concerts aroused orgiastic enthusiasm not unknown in revivalist meetings. The rhythm and emotional intensity of primitive religion were communicated in Presley's style, which harnessed black gospel and blues to white popular music. His controversial biographer Albert Goldman likened him to the charismatic shaman of a cult whose members believe themselves to be possessed by demons and by sickness:

To exorcize the demons and restore the 'sick' to their normal selves, the cult contrives through the use of inciting music and dance to arouse its members to a state of ecstasy. In this open condition, they can be freed of their demons through the ministrations of a charismatic shaman, who possesses the remarkable gift of taking the evil spirits into his own body and soul, where he either defeats them in combat or placates them by sweet offerings (1981, p. 257).

More clearly than in the case of most political or religious charismatics, Elvis Presley's character and the nature of his appeal may be linked with early trauma. His twin was stillborn at birth. His family was devastated by this loss. Their grief was compounded by the absences of the father who was either in jail or away at work for much of his childhood (Goldman, p. 87ff.). His mother spoke incessantly about the lost child. His soul, she believed, had passed into Elvis. She would set a place at table for the dead child. Her anxiety for Elvis, whom she 'worshipped', was so great that she did not let him play out of her sight until he was fifteen. Elvis' identification with the lost twin inclined him to the creation of a persona through which the lost child could symbolically live on. This persona was the basis of Elvis' stage character and of his charismatic appeal.

Among popular charismatics, the lives of John Lennon and Marilyn Monroe are documented in unusual detail. The origins and nature of their charismatic appeal are clearer than those of charismatic religious or political leaders. They give much insight into charisma in its various manifestations. John Lennon began as one of Elvis' 'believers': 'Nothing really affected me until Elvis,' he said (Davies, 1979, p. 35). Lennon's charisma also had semi-religious undertones, with undercurrents of childhood grief. He too identified himself with Jesus: 'I'd like to be like Christ . . . I think I'll win because I believe in what Jesus said' (Coleman, 1984, II 98, 109). At one time, he cultivated a Christ-like look, with gaunt, ascetic face and beard, and sang of being 'crucified'. Brought up in the church, Lennon kept a sense of the power of faith in society. He described himself as a Christian communist: 'If I could do what Christ did,' he said, 'be as Christ was, that's what being a Christian is all about. I try to live as Christ lived. It's tough, I can tell you' (*ibid.*, p. 112). Rock music to Lennon was in part a means of spiritual expression. With tactless sincerity, he compared his band with Jesus: 'We meant more to kids than Jesus' (*ibid.*, I 315).

Lennon's childhood was scarred by the trauma of his parents' separation, leading to his virtual adoption by his aunt (Coleman, 1984).

Immersed as a child in an intense fantasy life, he had moments of 'cosmic consciousness' not unlike those of mystics: 'I was always seeing things in a hallucinatory way. It was scary as a child because there was nobody to relate to . . . Surrealism to me is reality. Even as a child . . . I would find myself seeing hallucinatory images of my face changing and becoming cosmic and complete' (1981, p. 110). Consequently, Lennon felt that he belonged to the 'universe', not having belonged to a secure family:

> My mother was of the sky.
> My father was of the earth.
> But I am of the universe
> And you know what it's worth.
> 'Yer Blues'

In a similar way, Marilyn Monroe experienced a sensation of belonging to the universe as the first intimation of her charismatic appeal and of her later screen persona. In her ghosted autobiography, *My Life* (1974), she described herself at age sixteen on the beach:

> I paid no attention to the whistles and whoops. In fact, I didn't hear them. I was full of a strange feeling, as if I were two people. One of them was Norma Jean from the orphanage who belonged to nobody. The other was someone whose name I didn't know. But I knew where she belonged. She belonged to the ocean and the sky and the whole world (p. 25).

Belonging to nobody, she belonged to everyone and everything, for the Public was her only home:

> I belonged to the Public and to the world, not because I was talented or even beautiful but because I had never belonged to anything or anyone else. The Public was the only family, the only Prince Charming, and the only home I ever dreamed of (*ibid.*, p. 124).

Marilyn Monroe's admission that she belonged to the Public 'because I had never belonged to anything or anyone else' was literally true as she had been raised on public funds virtually from birth. Born Norma Jean Mortensen in Los Angeles in 1926, she never knew her father and hardly saw her mother who was an institutionalized schizophrenic. Until her first marriage at sixteen, she lived with a succession of families (nine in all, she claimed), and for about two years (1935–7), after her mother was confined to an asylum, she lived in a Los Angeles orphanage. Her charismatic appeal seems to have emanated from the aura of public availability which surrounded her and which she cultivated. Her orphanhood, wrote Arthur

Miller, 'heightened her charged presence' (1987, p. 306), and she wrote of herself:

> As I grew older I knew I was different from other children because there were no kisses or promises in my life. I often felt lonely and wanted to die. I would try to cheer myself up with daydreams. I never dreamed of anyone loving me as I saw other children loved. That was too big a stretch for my imagination. I compromised by dreaming of my attracting someone's attention (besides God), of having people look at me and say my name (1974, p. 16).

Her luscious persona belonging 'to the ocean and the sky and the whole world' was largely her own creation, the blend of sexual allure, wit and pathos the product of much calculation and art. She spent hours each day in front of mirrors with lipsticks, powders and mascara. 'There's not a single movement,' she said, 'not a single inflection in a line that I haven't learned by myself, working it over a thousand times' (Lembourn, 1979, pp. 16–17). She spoke of 'the face that I've made', a face and an image which she did not believe to be naturally beautiful but which she virtually willed into being. She transcended her roles, using them as showcases for moments of child-like wistful radiance, innocence and freshness. She was tragic and suggestive of unfathomable disturbance yet sweetened this image with physical beauty and the honey of sex. Her roles are memorable not for themselves as much as for her screen persona, and the fascination of her persona does not lie in the acting, fine as it often is, but in the hints of the real, vulnerable creature behind the mask.

Her marriages were a continuation of early patterns of attachment, suspicion and betrayal, with the difference that she could – and did – terminate each relationship. Her three husbands, and other men with whom she was involved, were considerably older than she. She sought in marriage the father whom she never had. As a child, she had fantasied that Clark Gable was her father. Later, she came to admire Abraham Lincoln and said that she thought of Lincoln as her father. Arthur Miller was 'Papa' to her. And her need for a father showed itself in many other ways. For example, in her first appearance on stage, in the New York Actors' Studio in 1956, she chose the part of Anna Christie in Eugene O'Neill's play and acted the opening scene in which Anna, a prostitute who has never known her father, is about to meet him for the first time since infancy. Her lifelong search for a father was part of the mystery of her appeal, but contrary to the impression projected on screen, there was often a deadening of feeling in her attachments to men. Grief, anxiety, anger – the emotional detritus of childhood – conspired to prevent her from loving. She recalled that already as a schoolgirl surrounded by admiring men, she had wanted to feel but could not: '... with all my lipstick and mascara and precocious curves, I was as unsensual as a fossil... I would have liked to want something as much as they did. I wanted nothing' (1974, pp. 26–7). As a grown woman, she came to see that her promiscuity had not led to the deepening of her attachments but, on the contrary, had numbed her like a drug: 'I sometimes felt I was hooked on sex, the way an alcoholic is on liquor or a junkie on dope. My body turned all these people on, like turning on an electric light, and there was so rarely anything human in it' (Weatherby, 1977, p. 146). Friends and acquaintances were often struck by the air of insulation which surrounded her. She sometimes gave the impression of being hidden behind a great wall of cotton. Arthur Schlesinger Jnr. described the 'terrible unreality' of talking with her, 'as if talking with someone under water'.

Belonging to the public, she found in the end the same fragmentation and the absence of consistent love that she had known as a child. In conversation, she would often describe herself using disturbing images of being cut to pieces, eaten up or disappearing. For example, she said, 'I sometimes feel as if I'm too exposed, I've given myself away, the whole of me, every part, and there's nothing left that's private, just me alone' (Weatherby, p. 127). She even intimated that the escape into make-believe was analogous to suicide: '... sometimes it seems you escape altogether and people never let you come back' (*ibid.*, p. 150). Only up to a point did her gifts enable her to transcend and master her childhood griefs; beyond that, they pointed the way to her suicide. In one of her recurring nightmares, she would run naked through a cemetery looking frantically for a way out. She dreamed of herself as a wilful Icarus bent on self-destruction: 'I dream of breaking out through the bars and soaring up, up, up... Sometimes at night I dream I become free and fly upward toward the sun and into it, so my wings burn off and I fall through the universe' (Lembourn, p. 56).

Lennon's charisma, too, was based partly on an appeal for help. He once admitted that his song 'Help' was an actual cry for help in the trough of depression: 'Now I may be very positive – yes, yes – but I also go through deep depressions where I would like to jump out of the window' (1981, p. 112). The causes of these depressions were not obscure: repeated losses in childhood, the concomitant feelings of abandonment, isolation and insecurity, of being emotionally crippled and in pain, of a distorted self-image. These feelings are explored repeatedly in Lennon's songs: '... creating is a result of pain... I have to put it somewhere and I write songs' (1980, p. 94). He believed that all creative people like himself are motivated by an appalling need for love and said that 'If I had the capabilities of being something other than I am, I would' (*ibid.*, p. 11).

Lennon's early childhood was chaotic. Until he was five it was not certain who would raise him. His parents were both musical, happy-go-lucky, and unstable, and their marriage was doomed from the start. The father, a waiter at sea, had married while on leave in Liverpool. He was rarely home and at the time of Lennon's birth in 1940, no one knew his whereabouts. The mother, despite her affection for her son, was disinclined or unable to care for him properly, especially when she became involved with another man. After an incident in which the father absconded with him to Blackpool and he was asked to choose between his father and mother, he hardly saw either parent. His mother lived only a short distance away, and he was always conscious of her existence: 'my feelings never died off for her' (Davies, p. 26). In the song 'Mother', he starkly laments his loss, 'you had me but I never had you'. In another song addressed to her, 'Julia', he writes: 'Half of what I say is meaningless/But I say it just to reach you, Julia.' Her sudden death in a car accident in 1958 when he was seventeen was an enormous blow. He described himself as being in a blind rage for about two years afterwards.

Nevertheless, conditions for Lennon after his parents' separation were fairly good. The strength which he derived from substitute mothering enabled him in later life to confront his trauma and try to master it:

> There were five women who were my family. Five strong, intelligent women. Five sisters. One happened to be my mother. My mother was the youngest. She just couldn't deal with life. She had a husband who ran away to sea and the war was on and she couldn't cope with me, and when I was four and a half, I ended up living with her elder sister. Now, these women were fantastic (1981, p. 110).

In retrospect, he felt that not having parents was a gift as well as an overwhelming trauma: 'I was free from the parents' stranglehold. That was the gift I got for not having parents. I cried a lot about not having them and it was torture, but it also gave me an awareness early' (*ibid.*).

The enormous number of styles and faces with which he experimented testify to the insecurity of his self-image, and his songs reflect this variety: in some he affirms a vision of universal harmony and love, but in others he emerges as vulgar, violent and cruel. Acutely conscious of being cut off from the world, Lennon was often aggrieved by his own egocentricity and aggressive ambition. Age, success, a relatively happy marriage and fatherhood mellowed him, but as a schoolboy and in his adolescence he had been delinquent, in his young manhood he came close to being an alcoholic and a drug addict, in his early married life he was at times unbearable, and he knew it: 'I am a violent man who has learned not to be violent and regrets his violence' (*ibid.*, p. 114).

Having been 'abandoned' by his father and having also lost his step-father when he was twelve, Lennon had a notorious need for and hatred of parental authority. In the absence of a strong father, he developed an unusually tough, aggressive 'macho' image with which to identify himself. Throughout much of his life, he was regularly attracted to parent-figures, such as the Maharishi, and he rejected them all in the end. (His song 'God' includes an entire litany of failed gods.) His anti-authoritarianism was an important facet of his appeal to the young during the 1960s and 1970s.* For him as for other charismatics, independence and originality were bound up with unresolved grief, depression and hostility toward parental authority: 'Daddy doesn't heal us,' he said. 'You have to heal yourself' (1981, p. 144).

It may be that his collaboration with Paul McCartney was determined by shared experiences of loss, especially as many of their songs tell openly of the effects of loss and separation and of the need for love. McCartney had shown relatively little interest in music before his mother died of cancer in 1956 when he became obsessed by the guitar (Davies, p. 44). According to his brother, Michael McCartney, after the death of Lennon's mother, 'John and Paul had a bond that went beyond even the music' (Coleman, 1984, I 91).

Among outstanding charismatic figures of popular entertainment, qualities similar to those found in religious and political leaders are often exagger-ated and are, therefore, especially clear. These include: a combination of weakness and strength, the creation of a new identity, and union with a mass audience. The weakness of charismatics such as Charlie Chaplin, Marilyn Monroe or John Lennon often springs from early family loss or deprivation, leading to low self-esteem, depression and the blockage of

---

* Anti-authoritarianism linked to childhood loss was apparently also part of the charisma of the film star James Dean in the 1950s. Dean's mother died of cancer when he was nine, and he felt himself to have been 'abandoned' by his father who was unable to raise him. In the post-war atmosphere of hysteria and repression caused by the American government-endorsed witch-hunt against Commun-ists, Dean could be 'adopted' by the Public as an apt representative of creative rebellion: 'Symbolizing the very ideas of individual rights and rebellion, he appealed to an entire generation of young people who adopted him as their hero' (Alexander, 1994, p. 4).

feeling. But the weakness does not predominate. In fact, it creates an urgent need to develop unusual strength in other areas. This strength is drawn from the positive conditions following the trauma, coupled with natural gifts and a creative outlet. In the struggle to overcome or to master his weaknesses, the charismatic artist uses the media to recreate himself, to enhance his worth in his own eyes and in the eyes of his society or nation or the entire world. Not having belonged to a secure home, he may find or create a home within an abstract entity such as the Public or the Universe. In the process of doing so, he splits off the new, magnetic being from the wounded, unwanted self. The new self, like the work of art which it creates or which is created by it, is a superstructure with a poor or nonexistent foundation. It belongs not to a secure family but to the ocean and the sky and the whole world.

8 Chaplin: Of Crime and Genius

Mr. Skimpole (of Ada Clare): We will not call such a lovely creature as that, who is a joy to all mankind, an orphan. She is the child of the universe.

Mr. Jarndyce: The world makes rather an indifferent parent, I am afraid.

Charles Dickens, Bleak House

Charlie Chaplin (1889–1977) made the essentials of his life story transparent in his art. The monumental rise from a London workhouse to a Hollywood studio, from abject poverty and dire neglect to limitless wealth, adoration and fame, the creation of enduring art out of the foul rag-and-bone shop of a melancholy Victorian childhood (it comes as no surprise that Chaplin greatly admired Dickens) – the main outline of Chaplin's life underlines his films and with the passage of time has virtually taken on the power of a myth.

Few would quarrel with Chaplin's place as the supreme master of film pantomime. As the creator of the best-known human character on film, he is virtually the only silent star who retains his universal appeal, particularly among children, and whose best films, in spite of their occasional naivety and maudlin sentimentality, are rarely equalled in their power to amuse and to move.

Chaplin's success, which coincided with the start of World War I, was so sudden and immense that he was quickly able to put himself out of the reach of studio vagaries, vicissitudes and rivalries which were to mar or ruin the careers of the Marx Brothers, Laurel and Hardy and, most tragically, Buster Keaton. He built his own studio, ruled it with a dictatorial hand, and made his films as much the exploration and expression of one man as possible. Through his films and his *Autobiography* (1964), we know Chaplin more intimately, perhaps, than any actor in the history of the cinema. Proust wrote that every artist has but one *oeuvre* – essentially Chaplin had one story in him. Each of his films tells, directly or obliquely, a fragment or variation of it. Some films, such as *The Kid* (1921) and *City Lights* (1930), tell bigger or more important chunks of the story than others and reveal with greater limpidity the main sources of Chaplin's creative urge. The hardest part of his story was kept until towards the end, in *The Great Dictator* (1940) and *Monsieur Verdoux* (1947). The psychological interest of these latter films is that when Chaplin abandoned the role of the Tramp and spoke for the first time on film, he chose to portray mass-murderers.

Though Chaplin hated and despised Hitler, he also felt a perverse kinship with the charismatic tyrant. He believed that the forces which had made him into a comedian and Hitler into a dictator were not dissimilar: 'Just think, he's the madman, I'm the comic,' he said at the time of making *The Great Dictator*. 'But it could have been the other way around' (Chaplin Jr., 1960, p. 180). Apart from the remarkable physical similarity and the fact that they were born in the same year, there were also the disrupted family backgrounds, the psychopathological tendencies, the need to control others, the unprecedented mass appeal, and above all the tremendous instinct for the theatrical. Chaplin, as we have seen, spoke of Hitler as 'the greatest actor of us all' (*ibid.*, p. 204). Hitler, too, was not unaware of the similarity and consequently banned Chaplin's films in Germany.

Chaplin's identification with the criminal is reflected on a smaller scale also in his next film, *Monsieur Verdoux*, which was begun at the height of the carnage of World War II. Based on a true story, it tells of a bank clerk who marries women for their money, then murders and incinerates them. In the end he is caught and brought to trial. Before being sentenced to death he argues his innocence by claiming that governments are in the business of mass murder – he is only a small entrepreneur.

Chaplin's role as the murderer was, nevertheless, foreshadowed in his Little Tramp character. The Tramp often shows signs of criminality, in his petty larcenies and his sadism which are part of his world of flophouses, grimy alleys, drunkenness, illness, cold and hunger. He is not above stealing from the blind or maltreating women and children. Chaplin's comedy, his pathos and loveability, obscure the fact that he is also one of the most cruel of comedians.

Chaplin's delinquent streak was present in childhood. In his *Autobiography*, he writes that after growing up in Edwardian England, he could understand the Teddy Boy of the 1950s, 'his attitude perhaps motivated by a subconscious feeling that man is only a half-tame animal who has for centuries governed others by deceit, cruelty and violence . . .' (p. 91). Chaplin saw himself as something of a 'half-tame animal', his creative urge having its roots partly in asocial impulses. According to his son,

Chaplin was once approached by gangsters who promised that if he ever needed someone bumped off all he had to do was to call them. He was delighted to find that 'many of these people in the underworld admire the creative principle' (Chaplin Jr., pp. 341–2).

One of the many facets of Chaplin's creativity lies in his unusual ability to free-associate, and spontaneously to juxtapose seemingly unconnected objects or incidents which, like the consecutive incidents in dreams, yield clues to the workings of the unconscious. Chaplin's *Autobiography* is by no means a conventional one in which events are related in consecutive order, though there is a rough chronological sequence. Often there are peculiar twists and jumps in time. In the strangest of these, the account of his mother's declining years is flanked on one side by his visit to Sing Sing penitentiary in the early 1920s, and on the other side by his argument that the criminal and the genius are similar by nature. Chaplin tells vividly of his horror at the inhuman conditions at Sing Sing, his memory of a man unjustly imprisoned, the sinister-looking electric chair. Then he describes his mother's last years in Santa Monica – he brought her over from England in 1921 and she lived in California until her death in 1928. Immediately after the account of her death, he returns to the early 1920s and gleefully relates a conversation that he had with the sculptress Clare Sheridan, who had made a bust of him: ' "This should be the bust of a criminal," I said. "On the contrary, it's the head of a genius." I laughed and developed a theory about the genius and the criminal being closely allied . . .' (p. 312).

The *Autobiography* opens not with Chaplin's birth but with the revelation that his mother went insane when he was a boy. Actually, she had been unstable for years and had spent time in an asylum several years previously.* At that time, Chaplin and Sydney (his older half-brother) had passed into the care of his father whom he hardly knew – father and mother had separated when Chaplin was one year old – but within a few months mother and children were reunited. The mother was committed again to an asylum, this time for over a year. Her tragedy, which occurred after the father's death, was apparently the critical event of Chaplin's early years. It marked the total break-up of his family and it forced Chaplin and his brother to fend for themselves. By the time the mother regained her sanity both were independent and Chaplin had begun his acting career. However, within a few years, when he was about sixteen and firmly established in the theatre, she suffered a relapse and spent the rest of her life in care. Parallel family circumstances are found in other film charismatics,

---

* Robinson (1985) has attempted to reconstruct the chronology.

as we have seen, notably Marilyn Monroe and Cary Grant, whose mothers were also institutionalized and their fathers absent.

'Motherless and fatherless – perhaps those words sum up the greatest lack my father felt in childhood,' wrote Charles Jr. (p. 10). The mother's insanity caused deep and lasting guilt, for Chaplin was at an age when he would have suspected or believed that he was somehow responsible. He never forgot her remark, 'If only you had given me a cup of tea . . . I would have been all right' (1964, p. 71); and he connected this with Joseph Conrad's remark that life made him feel like a cornered blind rat waiting to be clubbed. Was Chaplin's identification with the criminal, and even with Hitler, due in part to his exaggerated sense of guilt towards his mother? How do these latent forces of violence and guilt underlie his charisma?

Like many children in similar situations, Chaplin blamed not only himself but also his mother for having 'deserted' him. When she first went mad he was not yet eight, but had already spent over a year in workhouses and schools for orphans and destitute children, experiences which, no doubt, increased his ambivalence towards her. (The moment in *The Kid* when the child raised by the Tramp is torn from his arms and hauled off to an orphanage must owe some of its power to Chaplin's memory of being taken from his mother when he was sent to the Lambeth workhouse.) When his brother Sydney told him the news he could not believe it: 'I did not cry, but a baffling despair overcame me. Why had she done this? Mother, so lighthearted and gay – how could she go insane? Vaguely I felt that she had deliberately escaped from her mind and had deserted us' (*ibid.*, p. 24).

City Lights, Chaplin's most touching and intimate film, was begun soon after his mother's death in 1928. Its unprecedented pathos and conviction reflect Chaplin's mourning and his efforts to come to terms with his mother's insanity and to achieve restitution with her. The film is Chaplin's most accomplished fantasy of rescuing a woman in distress, a recurrent theme in his films. The Tramp falls in love with a blind flower-girl, luminous and impoverished, and allows her to believe that he is fabulously wealthy. He discovers by chance that an operation can restore her sight, and much of the film is a series of vignettes depicting his brilliantly comic and pathetic efforts to raise money for the operation. After obtaining the money and giving it to her, he is imprisoned for theft. By the time he is freed, the girl's sight has been restored and she has opened a flower shop. He passes the shop and gazes through the window. She does not recognize him, and he hurries on. But something about his intense look of longing impels her to run after him to press a flower and a coin into his hand. Of this scene, the film critic James Agee (1949) has written, 'It is enough to shrivel the heart to see, and it is the greatest piece of acting and the highest moment in movies. "You?" she asks. He nods, smiling shyly. "You can see now?" he asks. "Yes, I can see now."' (1963, II 10).

In an early draft of the story, described in the *Autobiography*, Chaplin was to play a clown blinded in a circus accident:

> He has a little daughter, a sick, nervous child, and when he returns from the hospital the doctor warns him that he must hide his blindness from her until she is well and strong enough to understand, as the shock might be too much for her. His stumblings and bumpings into things make the girl laugh joyously (p. 352).

As a child, Chaplin could not have understood clearly the nature of his mother's illness. These tragi-comic gropings could represent his own attempts to take on the burden of 'seeing', of understanding, and coming to terms with his consequent feelings of disablement, betrayal, guilt and violent anger. His salient methods of doing so are the synthesis of the comic and the tragic, and the splitting of the image of woman and of his own character. Whereas in the final version of *City Lights* the blind girl, the essence of idealization, is saved, in *Monsieur Verdoux* the women, with one exception, are abhorrent and are brutally murdered. It may be that by splitting the idealized and the despised image of woman and by presenting himself, on the one hand, as the romantic dreamer rescuing his beloved and, on the other hand, as the criminal uninhibited by moral restraints, Chaplin deals with his profound ambivalence towards his mother.

A memory of Chaplin's from the period of his mother's first return from the asylum is, no doubt, a screen memory representing a whole aspect of his childhood and personality, and particularly his terror at the collapse of whatever childhood security he had known. He himself suspected that this incident might have anticipated the premise of his films – the combination of the comic and the tragic:

> At the end of our street was a slaughterhouse, and sheep would pass our house on their way to be butchered. I remember one escaped and ran down the street, to the amusement of onlookers. Some tried to grab it and others tripped over themselves. I had giggled with delight at its lambent capering and panic, it seemed so comic. But when it was caught and carried back into the slaughterhouse, the reality of the tragedy came over me and I ran indoors, screaming and weeping to Mother, 'They're going to kill it! They're going to kill it!' (p. 31).

Soon after his mother's return from the asylum, when he was not yet nine, Chaplin was apprenticed to a travelling group of clog-dancers. Though he must have been lonely, depressed, and anxious, he does not mention this and does not write of missing his mother. Instead, he lists various English comedians who committed suicide. Difficult as it was to live without his mother, it was probably even harder to live with her. On returning home, he developed severe asthma, and his mother withdrew him from the troupe. His strangling home life, 'a quagmire of miserable circumstances' (p. 43), might have been expressed in this symptom – for months, Chaplin writes, he could hardly breathe and at times he wanted to end it all by jumping out of the window.

Despite the vividness of Chaplin's account of these early years, there are notable blank spots, and much of the *Autobiography* is sketchy and unreliable. Most significantly, Chaplin's mother remarried and had two children between her stays in the asylum (1898–1903), but Chaplin omits this completely. Also, he describes the grand funeral of his father in 1901, whereas in fact he was buried in a pauper's grave. In real life as in his portrayal of the Tramp, Chaplin denied the full extent of his degradation. Nevertheless, despite its unreliability, the *Autobiography* is unusually revealing of the psychology of the charismatic. It gives the background of his public persona and his triumphs as an extreme sense of chaos and unpredictability in childhood, abrupt shifts in fortune, the suffering and pity, and a desperate need to master trauma through his gifts. It is no wonder that in later life, as Charles Jr. writes, 'He was happiest, most comfortable, when things were the same, when you rose in the morning with the certainty of what you were going to do at four in the afternoon' (p. 75).

Critics such as Raoul Sobel and David Francis are mistaken in playing down the effects of Chaplin's early experiences on his later development:

> Poverty when it came, only lasted three or four years, after which he was in almost continuous work. Even the workhouse and orphanage he was sent to would have been nothing as terrifying as at the beginning of Victoria's reign. They supplied meat and fresh milk every day and provided a balanced diet many poor people nowadays would be grateful to receive. Of course, there must have been periods of near-starvation when his mother was in the asylum and his brother at sea; moments of despair, of loneliness, hopelessness, of biting shame, but they did not last forever (1977, pp. 63–4).

Research in child development (Bowlby, 1969–80) leaves no doubt that the disruption of Chaplin's bond with his mother was at least as important as their poverty, though the material and the emotional sufferings were linked. According to Chaplin's son, he confessed a source of deeper hurt than poverty, 'a feeling that his mother had failed him when he had needed her most' (p. 10).

The material poverty 'did not last forever', but to the child it probably seemed forever. The sense of being emotionally impoverished, expressed in the character of the Tramp, stayed with Chaplin long after he became a millionaire and the most famous man in the world. Certain traits – his extreme shyness (Stan Laurel, who knew him well, said that he was 'desperately shy'), his 'romantic hunger' (his own phrase); his instability; his fierce independence; his submissiveness; his 'colossal ego' (as Charles Jnr. called it); his love of power; his lack of self-confidence; his compulsive acquisition of wealth; his many difficulties in human relationships – originated, at least in part, in the unstable and eventually disrupted childhood bonds.

Though Chaplin's main troubles clearly lay with his mother and he hardly saw his father except for the brief time after his mother's first breakdown, the father – and his absence – strongly influenced his view of human behaviour and relationships. His father was quiet and easy-going when sober, but violent when drunk. (To the end of his life, Chaplin remembered that whenever his mother was angry with him, she would say, 'You'll end up in the gutter like your father' [1964, p. 8].) Men in Chaplin's films appear to embody a split of this sort. In *The Gold Rush*, the Tramp's companion, a friend in normal circumstances, literally tries to eat him when they are starving; and in *City Lights*, the Tramp's millionaire friend offers to help him when drunk but cannot remember him when sober.

Like his father, Chaplin was given to abrupt shifts in mood, and had a volcanic temper which sometimes erupted at the least provocation. Charles Jnr. witnessed many of these outbursts as a child, and remembered how frightened he had been. His mother, Chaplin's second wife, Lita Grey, was a frequent target of Chaplin's hysterical tirades during their short, stormy marriage in the mid-1920s. Chaplin's cameraman, Roland Totheroh, corroborates these recollections:

He got in the bathroom and if the door wouldn't open, he'd pull the handles off the door. He broke windows and everything else up there when he'd go into a tantrum. That's why he had Dr. Reynolds [a psychiatrist and close friend of Chaplin's]. He always figured he was going to go insane (Lyons, 1972, p. 283).

This irrational rage and the fear of insanity help to explain Chaplin's identification with Hitler, whom he regarded as a madman.

At other times, Chaplin would lapse into severe depressions which had apparently plagued him since childhood. He was remembered by neighbours and friends in London as a very quiet child who would suddenly erupt with absurd bursts of gaiety. The atmosphere which he calls up in his childhood recollections is strikingly like that in some of his films. He writes of his life at the schools for orphans: 'It was a forlorn existence. Sadness was in the air' (p. 20). The days after his mother went insane for the first time, when he lived with his father and his father's dissipated mistress, were 'the longest and saddest of my life' (p. 26). His memories of the furniture and decoration in his father's house indicate his depressed, morbid state: 'The wallpaper looked sad, the horsehair furniture looked sad, and the stuffed pike in a glass case that had swallowed another pike as large as itself – the head sticking out of its mouth – looked gruesomely sad . . .' (pp. 24–5).

During his mother's second bout of mental illness, when she was occasionally so violent that she had to be kept in a padded room (McCabe, 1978, p. 44), Chaplin was on tour in a production of *Sherlock Holmes*. At this time, he recalled in his *Autobiography*, he was severely withdrawn and depressed:

> I got accustomed to living alone. But I got so much out of the habit of talking that when I suddenly met a member of the company I suffered intense embarrassment. I could not collect myself quickly enough to answer questions intelligently, and they would leave me, I am sure, with alarm and concern for my reason (p. 79).

Later, after he joined Fred Karno's vaudeville company, there were a number of occasions when Karno was ready to dismiss him as his brooding presence offstage had such a demoralizing effect on the rest of the company. On stage, however, he was Karno's leading comedian. Afterwards, when he became famous in pictures, his depression, isolation, and loneliness did not end: 'I had always liked the public's attention, and here it was – paradoxically isolating me with a depressing sense of loneliness' (*ibid.*, p. 187).

In later years, too, depression was a frequent visitor. According to Lita Grey Chaplin, 'news of the death of someone he didn't know but simply admired, could hurl him into the depths of depression' (1966, p. 219). Charles Jnr. recalled that when his father was depressed he became very quiet:

> Anything might bring on these spells – even the account of a tragedy in the newspaper could upset him – but they usually visited him when

he felt deserted by the creative impulse, when he would wait in vain for ideas that wouldn't come. It was as though he were bound hand and foot in some dark dungeon of the soul (p. 99).

It is likely that Chaplin, in common with other charismatics such as Churchill, needed to work in order to ward off depression. For this reason, he was most affected when unable to work. An acquaintance, Jim Tully, wrote that Chaplin's favourite story was that of Joseph Grimaldi, the famous English-Italian clown who was so sad that he went to a doctor. 'I recommend that you see Grimaldi.' To which the poor man replied, 'I am Grimaldi' (1943, pp. 21–2).

In common with Churchill, Chaplin's acquaintanceship with despair gave him unusual sources of creative fortification – the serious, tragic premise of his comedy, which struck a chord worldwide, especially in the years 1914–45. Chaplin had an extraordinary gift of stimulating feeling, of buoying the spirits, of taking people outside themselves. This he learned while perfecting his art from a prolonged inner struggle against depression, which became an integral part of his charismatic bond with his audience.

Chaplin himself knew all too well that his depression and rage sprang partly from the bond with the mother and her insanity. The pathos of this bond lay in the apparent fact that although she was an adoring and an adored mother, he could not bear her. In her last years he could not see her without plunging into depression:

> I'm so thrown off when I go to see her that I can't create, I can't function, for days. I know she's not in pain, but when I look at her, when I remember how beautiful and gay she once was, when I see how her mind's not working, I get too upset. It's best that I keep away from her unless it's absolutely necessary that I go to her (Lita Grey Chaplin, p. 229).

Charles Jnr. wrote that his father 'could never see her without feeling a depression that was sometimes as acute to him as physical pain that would last for days afterwards, preventing all concentration on his work' (p. 16).

Already during his adolescence, a quarter-century earlier, Chaplin found it almost impossible to live with his mother. He remembered fighting back depression when they lived together for the last time, for a few weeks when he was about fourteen: 'Poor Mother, who wanted so little out of life to make her gay and cheerful, reminded me of my unhappy past – the last person in the world who should have affected me this way' (1964, p. 82). Shortly after, she was returned to the asylum, and the medical certificate for her contains a statement of Chaplin's which gives an idea of the torment which he suffered: 'she keeps on mentioning a lot of people and fancies she can see them looking out of the window and talking to imaginary people – going into strangers' rooms etc.' (Robinson, 1985, p. 40).

Chaplin's ambivalence towards his mother was the more difficult for him to bear because he regarded her as his greatest teacher and attributed to her his genius at pantomine. Anthony Asquith's praise of Chaplin is universally acknowledge as true:

> I have never known anyone to compare with him in the power to make real and vivid a person he has met or an incident he has seen in the street. It was not a question of mimicry or verbal description, it was an act of creation. He, himself, disappeared, leaving a kind of ectoplasm from which the people, the setting, event, materialized (Minney, 1954, p. 108).

Chaplin acquired this gift from his mother who at one time was a successful music-hall star. In his description of her unrealized artistic genius there are poignant hints of her illness:

> I learned from her everything I know. She was the most astounding mimic I ever saw. She would stay at the window for hours, gazing at the street and reproducing with her hands, eyes and expression all that was going on down there, and never stopped. It was in watching and observing her that I learned not only to translate motions with my hands and features, but also to study mankind. She was a far greater artist than I will ever be. She gave me all she had and asked nothing in return (*ibid.*, p. 6).

Still, this very gift and the success which it brought were sources of conflict, for Chaplin knew he had paid a heavy price. After his mother arrived in the United States, she asked him, 'Wouldn't you rather be yourself than live in this theatrical world of unreality?' He replied, 'You're responsible for this unreality.' (1964, p. 309)

Other revealing anecdotes about Chaplin's mother suggest that in her last years, though her needs were fully cared for, her life was rooted in the past, when hunger and danger were part of everyday life:

> Once when Syd went to see her, she went into the dining-room and brought him an apple and some oranges. 'Slip these in your pocket,' she said, 'You might get hungry. You'll need them.' On another occasion, when the doctor was round, he referred to her brilliant sons. 'They are both doing so well. Everybody is talking of them,' he said, but she just

looked at him blankly and replied: 'I have no sons.' 'But, Mrs. Chaplin, I'm talking of Charlie – and of Syd. Why they are world-famous. You must be very proud of them.' 'I have no children,' she repeated. After the doctor had gone, the nurse asked: 'Why did you say that, Mrs. Chaplin? Both the boys are here so often.' 'Well,' she said, 'I don't know what might have happened. They might be in some sort of trouble. Somebody may be after them' (Minney, p. 129).

According to Lita Grey Chaplin, whenever Chaplin's mother picked up her grandchildren, Charles Jr. or Sydney, Chaplin would become visibly alarmed. He was terrified that she might suddenly do something dangerous or criminal, such as drop them out of the window. (Charles Jr. relates that Chaplin himself would never pick him up as a child – perhaps he was afraid of similar madness in himself.) In the *Autobiography*, Chaplin tells of an incident at an ostrich farm where his mother snatched an ostrich egg from an attendant, saying, 'Give it back to the poor bloody ostrich' (p. 309), and tossed it into the corral where it exploded. Though this is told as an amusing story, it also illustrates symbolically the tragic instability which could lead her inadvertently to hurt her own children when trying to help them.

Yet Chaplin's ability to empathize with his mother's suffering, despite his own pain, accounts in no small measure for his art being ultimately an affirmation of life. As he sat beside her on her death-bed in 1928, 'a flood of memories surged in upon me of her lifelong struggle, her courage and her tragic, wasted life . . . and I wept' (*ibid.*, p. 311). It is true that he follows this up by writing of the affinities between the genius and the criminal. He hints at his own criminally violent and guilty impulses towards his mother, which found indirect expression in his films, especially *Monsieur Verdoux*. But then he asserts his faith in a manner which suggests that, in common with other charismatic public figures, his appeal has more to do with religion, however unorthodox, than might be thought:

The ways of life and death . . . may seem futile and meaningless . . . My faith is in the unknown, in all that we do not understand by reason; I believe that what is beyond our comprehension is a simple fact in other dimensions, and that in the realm of the unknown there is an infinite power of good (pp. 313–14).

Though Chaplin's bond with his mother was not so disturbed that it led him to feel that life was uncompromisingly futile and meaningless, it did help to blight most of his attachments to women. He needed maternal affection, but as he was terribly insecure and had to be in control he was particularly drawn to very young women who adored him and whom he could manipulate. Three of his four wives were teen-aged girls. But the last, Oona O'Neill (the daughter of Eugene O'Neill), gave him the under-standing, the security, the affection and the happiness (not to speak of eight children!) which he had always sought. This marriage lasted for over thirty years, until his death in 1977. Prior to this, his married life had been largely a sordid mess. Lita Grey Chaplin reported him as saying at the time of his marriage to Oona in 1943: 'I never understood women. I mistrusted them. When they got too close I conquered them, but I couldn't love them for long because I was convinced they couldn't love me' (p. 314).

Chaplin's idealization of women in his films was entirely autobio-graphical, a measure of his need to keep women at a distance and of his wish for reassurance in his chronic dependence. Stan Laurel has said that from childhood he was 'always expecting to meet the beautiful princess who would fall in love with him as deeply as he fell in love with her, and then they'd live happily ever after' (McCabe, 1978, p. 226). Chaplin him-self put it like this: when he was a young man, 'no woman could measure up to that vague image I had in my mind' (1964, p. 165). Of his first love, when he was sixteen, he wrote: 'I began to sink further into the hopeless mire of silent love. I hated this weakness and was furious with myself for lack of character. It was an ambivalent affair. I both hated and loved her' (p. 88). When he was nineteen he proposed impetuously to a chorus girl whom he had taken out a handful of times. When they broke up, he said, 'Already, you have too much of a power over me' (p. 107). Laurel described this girl as the first of Chaplin's 'little fairy princesses'. It is remarkable that when Chaplin came back to London in 1921, some twelve years later, his thoughts were still apparently focused on her, and he wanted to see her more than anyone else. Chaplin's homecoming was a moment of charis-matic frenzy comparable with that of Lenin in 1917 or Hitler in 1938 during his triumphal victory procession through the villages of Austria to Vienna (though without the violence of the former or the bloodlust of the latter). It was, in fact, as Robinson points out, 'an international celebration of idolatry which can be seen as the very peak of Chaplin's phenomenal popularity' (1983, p. 52). Yet Chaplin turned away from this mass adula-tion: 'This worship does not belong to me,' he wrote at the time in *My Trip Abroad* (1922, p. 60). On hearing that his former love had died – no matter that he had hardly known her – he felt that 'the bottom had fallen out of my world.'

Not long after his return to the United States, Chaplin started work in *A Woman of Paris* – at this time, too, he brought his mother over. This film is notable, among other things, for being the only one in which he explores a disturbed attachment of mother and son as a contributory cause of the son's troubles with an idealized woman. In the film, which Chaplin wrote and directed but did not star in, a young artist shares a studio apartment in Paris with his mother. He proposes to a woman whom he remembers and loves as the innocent country girl who was once his fiancée. However, since coming to Paris, she has become the mistress of a rich, charming voluptuary. His mother overhears the proposal and talks him out of it. The next evening, racked with despair, he commits suicide. In this and other films Chaplin seems to be exploring territory to which his psychopathology led him, but he never went so far in real life – perhaps partly because his films were cathartic. *Monsieur Verdoux*, which Chaplin regarded as his best film, appears to have satisfied most completely feelings which derived from the break-up of his family and his mother's madness: his sadistic impulses towards women, his ruthless drive for worldly success, his need to assert his innocence, and his masochism in assuaging his guilt (Verdoux being in the end condemned to death).

And so, when Chaplin said *a propos* his similarity to Hitler, 'it could have been the other way around' (Chaplin Jr., p. 180), he meant it. His inner world was in some ways not unlike Hitler's, especially in its intense idealism and violent potential. His charismatic appeal, likewise, might be attributed in part to the correspondence between his psychopathology and external reality, especially in the years 1914–45. Yet the criminality and violence in Chaplin's films are tempered by comedy and pathos which make bearable the harsh realities which he confronts: orphanhood and separation (*The Kid*); murder, cannibalism, greed (*The Gold Rush*); suicide, blindness (*City Lights*). Chaplin had more than a glimpse of the lower depths of human existence. His understanding of the hideous effects of his childhood, which he regarded as symptomatic of a general social malaise, is vivid in his films. Yet, in all his great pictures, redemption through love is finally, if shakily, achieved. To this must be attributed their astonishing, living humanity.

Conclusion

My interest in charisma was strongly affected by an unusual experience which I had as a trainee in child psychotherapy at the Tavistock Clinic, London, in 1980–82. As part of my training, I worked in a series of nurseries and children's homes in Oxford and London. For a short time, I worked simultaneously in two nurseries, both for children between 3–5. These nurseries were worlds apart: one mostly for children of single parents, run by the London Borough of Barnet, the other a private nursery in which almost all the children had both parents. In the borough nursery, I was needed, I would say desperately at times, by children who in many cases had no father. The children's endless demands exhausted and distressed me, though I found the work rewarding. A short bus ride took me to the private nursery. There the children mostly played among themselves, leaving the staff to supervise in the background. In attempting to analyze the enormous difference between the two nurseries, I connected the demands of the single-parent children in the borough nursery with their need for parenting. Later, when I began to think seriously about the phenomenon of charismatic appeal, I concluded that in adult life these children might be especially vulnerable in time of crisis to charismatic relationships, as leaders or as followers. In contrast, the children in the private nursery had no comparable needs or demands. They seemed content, to paraphrase Pascal, to play in their room. Their main interests were private, with one another.

At this time, in 1981, the marriage of the Prince of Wales and Diana Spencer stirred up the most intense charismatic outburst in Britain since the coronation. I was struck by the fact that Lady Diana came from a background typical of the children in the borough nursery, her parents having divorced when she was a child. I was then immersed in study of John Bowlby's monumental *Attachment and Loss*, which he had just finished, and was myself, with Bowlby's encouragement, writing a book on creative responses to childhood loss. Working with children from broken homes, I was strongly aware of Bowlby's observation that such children frequently repeat the pattern of family disruption in adult life. I suspected that the same might happen in the royal family, and that the fairy tale ambience of the wedding, though immensely appealing, was ominous. Perhaps only someone like Lady Diana, who had not had secure familial love and care in childhood, could attract and welcome such an overwhelming public role. In the end, as in the case of many charismatics, the pattern of private life was indeed repeated in public life. This image of public ideals and charismatic adulation coupled with private trauma (which has become painfully public) haunts these pages.

This book was written not as a theoretical study alone, but also for practical application: for example, in analyzing why a society chooses certain leaders at certain times, in interpreting the socio-psychological bases of international conflict, in explaining the symbolic value of charismatic phenomena, and in assessing the long-term effects on a society of a high divorce rate and incidence of single parent families.

Three basic forms of charisma have been explored – in politics, religion and the media – as well as a number of individual representatives of each. Through this Gestalt approach, using a combination of biography, history, sociology, religion and psychology, a new picture emerges of the nature and background of charisma. In its broadest sense, charisma is defined here as a relationship which comes about with the intersection of the traumatized inner world of the charismatic and external social and political crisis.

Charisma under objective intellectual scrutiny is inevitably seen as a form of psychopathology. In its context, however, it is normal. Even when viewed as aberration, however, charisma helps clarify the nature of normality; for pathology, as Freud (1933) pointed out, 'by making things larger and coarser, can draw our attention to normal conditions which would otherwise have escaped us' (p. 58). Charisma throws into relief the primary human need for love, care, and security in childhood family life.

Hinging as it does on the relativity of morality and pathology, charisma brings to mind the rabbinic paradox on the mysterious red heifer in Numbers 19: 'it purifies the impure and makes impure the pure.' A number of characteristics have been shown as frequent if not inevitable parts of charisma in all its forms. The public identity of the charismatic is created *faute de mieux*, in the absence of a secure and satisfactory private self. The charismatic is driven by trauma, usually in the form of a broken or disrupted childhood, which has no cure or solace except symbolically in the public domain. The Public becomes a substitute ideal of familial union and harmony, a substitute reality of breakdown and disillusionment. The charismatic needs social crisis to bring the external world into line with his pathology. When this correspondence is achieved, in conflict, pain and volatility, the charismatic bond becomes viable. The strength of this relationship depends in part on the Public's deflection from the charismatic's distorted inner self and the potential for disaster onto the selfish question: what can he do for me? In its purest forms, charisma transforms politics, religion and the media into art, disguising and sweetening the risk.

Most studies of charisma are from the public viewpoint. This book assesses the nature of charisma from the charismatic's point of view. I believe that charismatic phenomena are at root undesired by the charismatic. Given the choice as a child faced, for example, with maternal loss, he would hurl aside the prospect of creative achievement and fame as absurd recompense. (This, of course, is an extreme form of trauma: it may be surmised that lesser traumas – coupled with parallel strengths – promote varying degrees of unwilling charisma.) Only later, once the trauma is a *fait accompli*, does the political charismatic come to believe that trauma was a side-effect of his Destiny to lead, the religious charismatic that the trauma was part of a divine plan, and the charismatic entertainer that the trauma may be a divine gift, if harnessed creatively. Human nature especially in childhood gravitates to satisfaction and equilibrium in family life. Only if this fails, whether for internal or external reasons, does public life exert magnetic pull. While the sacrifice of private life is, to a degree, an inescapable consequence of public crisis, a *preference* for public over private life, even when such crisis does not exist, is an aberrant feature of charisma.

The view taken here is that in political and religious charisma the public identity must overshadow the private self. The charismatic relationship in religion and politics can succeed only through uncritical faith in the charismatic as a Public being. History teaches that a society in crisis cannot be overly concerned with the charismatic's personal origins and motives. It is either in too much pain or knows too little, or both, to analyze effectively the relationship and its possible consequences. In doing so, it would risk destroying the charismatic bond and its chances of ecstasy and salvation. However, in the most highly educated, politically stable and economically successful societies since the end of World War II and the start of the nuclear age, charisma has inevitably attracted such analysis, arousing as it does an unprecedented degree of wariness and fear. Hitler in particular has left a lasting distrust of charisma.

In contrast, media charismatics are 'safe'. They do not generally try to lead or to teach or impose a system of beliefs or government or a pattern of behaviour. They can feel free, and are often expected, not to take themselves too seriously. Our faith in them need not be absolute but, as in Coleridge's definition of poetry, is at most a willing suspension of disbelief. One could be a 'believer' in Paderewski or a 'worshipper' of Sarah Bernhardt, or more recently of Elvis or Marilyn Monroe, without having to believe totally or to sacrifice anything. The attraction of non-committal media charisma is all the greater as it is cheap and available and, in addition, it fills a void left by the decline of religious faith and of political charisma. The most serious of the media charismatics struggle to lay bare their inner world, usually in film and music. Their ultimate goal is the confession, exploration and catharsis of the traumatic sources of their mass appeal. In my view, the same is true of political and religious charismatics, except that they admit it at risk of losing their authority. (This risk, however, appears to be diminishing in Western societies in which religion and politics are often treated as branches of the media, whose authority is hardly binding.) The persona or 'new self' of the media charismatic is exposed in the art which is its vehicle and screen. Controlled divulgence of the truth about him does not necessarily undermine his spell. On the contrary, in some cases the more the Public knows the more it understands the art and the richer that art can become.

In ways not previously recognized, charisma is bound up with grief and mysticism. Like the mystic, the charismatic creates a new identity out of the ashes of a damaged or ruined self. The love or esteem of the Public is sought as a replacement for the love of individuals. In politics, the charismatic may use crisis to come to power, but the Public harnesses and utilizes the charismatic's dependence upon it. In exchange, it sacrifices some degree of control over its destiny. An element of risk is vital in the political and religious charismatic relationship, especially amid economic collapse and political upheaval. This gambling – for this is what charisma is at its core – assuages depression and offers hope, however temporarily, with an attractive (in these desperate circumstances) suicidal threat. In some cases, charismatic relationships involve collusion in criminality, justified in the name of God, or racial theories, or *realpolitik*, and packaged in art. As we have seen, charisma is closely linked with impulses and actions which in normal conditions would be socially unacceptable or illegal. The art of charisma creates a hypnotic spell by which morality is redefined: it is what Nietzsche called a transvaluation of values.

'Let him come. But don't let me see him' (*Sanhedrin* 98b). Rabbinic ambivalence to the most extreme form of charisma – messianic redemption – was expressed pithily in this way after the bloody failure of the Bar Kokhba revolt of the Jews against the Romans in 132–5 CE. This saying sums up the paradoxical nature of charismatic leadership of all forms and intensities throughout history. On the one hand, there is more awareness than ever of the importance of the stable family, of ethical values which are part of family life and education. On the other hand, with disconcerting regularity, large numbers of people continue to be drawn precisely to those who have no secure model of family life in their private lives, the artistry of whose appeal is propaganda for amorality.

Why? A number of explanations, each dependent on circumstances, emerge in this book, and a few of these may be summed up here. One possibility may lie in the breakdown of the family in Western society, the high rate of divorce and their effects on the children of these broken marriages. It may be that those from such homes best understand the need for stability and, therefore, are best able to create or promote these things, if not in their own lives then in the life of their society or nation. Still, as we have seen, it is sobering to reflect that charismatics thrive in conditions which recreate the instability and breakdown which they have known in private life. Perhaps equally true is that the Public is bonded to the charismatic because it responds humanly to the subtext of appeal – the cry for help. The charismatic, needing and craving a public role to find solutions nonexistent in private life, cultivates with ruthless singlemindedness public attractiveness and gifts which stimulate this bond. In other words, the Public, knowingly or not, is swindled. Potential non-charismatic leaders who might have greater ability and a more stable sense of self, a clearer perception of the needs of a society, and the capacity to mold it into a healthier self-image, have less need for and less interest in such a role. This is the Catch-22 of public life and of government.

A view of government which emerges from this interpretation of charisma is that healthy government does not draw undue concern to itself but breeds confidence in its functioning much as bodily health promotes forgetfulness of the body. The failure of bonding within the family and consequent social alienation may stimulate greater awareness of society and promote the bonding of the charismatic within an unstable society in crisis. Social psychologists have observed in normal families a process of negative imprinting which, in effect, acts as a buffer to incestuous relations. Incest is more likely when negative imprinting fails, through bereavement, separation or distortion of familial bonds. The projection of such a failed bond onto a similarly troubled society may be seen as a form of incest tenable during crisis but unviable in the long run: again, societies, like individuals, gravitate to health. In the short term, charisma may have a stabilizing effect, much as a rickety building may be strengthened by a huge weight placed on top of it, which can also bring the structure down.

At worst, submission to a charismatic bond may express pure self-destructiveness. Yet charisma is one of the strongest agents of symbolic immortality possessed by the human race. Biologically, human beings are incapable of living for long without the stress of crisis. The charismatic understands this need instinctively and is best able to tolerate and exploit it as he or she generally has a higher pain threshold and less of a private life to lose than others. Perhaps at times there is some deep-rooted wish to anticipate cathartically by means of the charismatic a potential trauma, to be inoculated against it, as it were. In some societies, charisma may be cultivated as an insurance against more virulent, less controllable strains of charisma which might appear, whether locally or elsewhere.

For some forms of charisma, there may be simpler explanations: a wish for stimulus amid depression, for the roller-coaster of artificial thrills which, in politics at least, holds out an attractive element of risk; or rebellion against social regimentation and anonymity, against the waste wild land of the undeveloped country or the comfortable zoo which industrial society may be perceived as becoming.

It may also be, finally, that the paradox of charisma involves an unremitting dynamism of stability and change, in which the concept of motive is irrelevant and that of fault morally neutral. This is simply how things are: charisma lies in the fault line of human affairs, an indication of powerful forces to which humanity has limited access and control, producing change, for good as well as for evil.

Charisma can be a force for evil, but it also represents that part of human nature which keeps alive primeval wildness and freedom. To frame its fearful symmetry is to strangle it. In the end, charisma is uncatchable, stalking invisibly, watching contemptuously the foolish consistencies of plodding politicians and petty bureaucrats, the routine torment of inefficiency, red tape and paltry corruption, waiting for the moment that will set it free.

Bibliography

ABERBACH, David (1981) 'On Re-reading Bialik: Paradoxes of a "National Poet" ' *Encounter* LVI 6: 41–8.

ABERBACH, David (1982) 'Loss and Separation in Bialik and Wordsworth' *Prooftexts* II 2: 197–208.

ABERBACH, David (1983) 'Charlie Chaplin: Of Crime and Genius' *Encounter* LX 5: 86–92.

ABERBACH, David (1984) 'Childlessness and the Waste Land in C.N. Bialik and T.S. Eliot' *Hebrew Union College Annual* LV 283–307.

ABERBACH, David (1985) 'Hitler's Politics and Psychopathology' *Encounter* LXV 3: 74–7.

ABERBACH, David (1988) *Bialik* (London: Peter Halban; New York: Grove Press).

ABERBACH, David (1989) *Surviving Trauma: loss, literature and psycho-analysis* (New Haven and London: Yale University Press).

ABERBACH, David (1993) 'Grief and Mystical Union: the Baal Shem Tov and Krishnamurti' *Harvard Theological Review* LXXXVI 3: 309–21.

ABERBACH, David (1995) 'Charisma and Attachment Theory: A Cross-disciplinary Interpretation' *International Journal of Psycho-Analysis* 76(4): 845–55.

AGEE, James (1949) 'Comedy's Greatest Era' In *Agee on Film*, Vol. 1, 1963.

ALEXANDER, Paul (1994) *James Dean: Boulevard of Broken Dreams* (London: Little, Brown & Co.).

ALGAR, Hamid (1985) Introduction to Ruhollah Khomeini, *Islam and Revolution: Writings and Declarations* (London: Routledge).

BERLIN, Isaiah (1982) *Personal Impressions* (Oxford University Press).

BENSMAN, J., and M. GIVANT (1975) 'Charisma and Modernity: The Use and Abuse of a Concept' *Social Research* 42(4): 570–614.

BIALIK, Chaim Nachman (1935) *Speeches* (Hebrew), 2 vols. (Tel Aviv: Dvir).

BIALIK, Chaim Nachman (1937–9) *Letters* (Hebrew) F. Lachower, ed. 5 vols. (Tel Aviv: Dvir).

BIALIK, Chaim Nachman (1955) *Letters to His Wife* (Hebrew and Yiddish). (Tel Aviv: Mossad Bialik and Dvir).

BIALIK, Chaim Nachman (1958) *Collected Works* (Hebrew). 19th edn. (Tel Aviv: Dvir).

BIALIK, Chaim Nachman (1971) *Posthumous Works* (Hebrew). M. Ungerfeld, ed. (Tel Aviv: Dvir).

BIALIK, Chaim Nachman (1973, orig. 1923) *Aftergrowth* (an extract). Tr. D. Patterson. *Jewish Quarterly* XX 4: 17–8. A full English translation appears in *Aftergrowth and other stories*, tr. I.M. Lask (Philadelphia: Jewish Publication Society, 1939).

BION, Wilfred (1961) *Experiences in Groups* (London: Tavistock Publications).

BOFF, Leonardo (1985, orig. 1981) *Church, Charisma and Power: Liberation Theology and the Institutional Church*. Tr. John W. Diercksmeier (London: SCM Press).

BOWLBY, John (1969, 1973, 1980) *Attachment and Loss*, 3 vols. (London: The Hogarth Press and The Institute of Psychoanalysis).

BRANDON, Ruth (1991) *Being Divine: A Biography of Sarah Bernhardt* (London: Secker & Warburg).

BRAUDY, Leo (1986) *The Frenzy of Renown: Fame and Its History* (New York, Oxford: Oxford University Press).

BROGAN, D.W. (1935) *Abraham Lincoln* (London: Duckworth).

BUBER, Martin (1964, orig. 1913) *Daniel: Dialogues of Realization*. Tr. M. Friedman (New York, Chicago, San Francisco: Holt, Rinehart and Winston).

BUBER, Martin (1970, orig. 1923) *I and Thou* (Ich und Du). Tr. W. Kaufmann (Edinburgh: T. & T. Clark).

BULLOCK, Alan (1986, orig. 1952) *Hitler: a study in tyranny* (Harmondsworth: Penguin Books).

BULLOCK, Alan (1960) *The Life and Times of Ernest Bevin*, vol. 1: *Trade Union Leader 1881–1940* (London: Heinemann).

BULLOCK, Alan (1991) *Hitler and Stalin* (New York: Alfred A. Knopf).

BUTTERFIELD, Herbert (1962, orig. 1939) *Napoleon* (London: Duckworth).

CARR, Edward (1978) *Hitler: A Study of Personality and Politics* (London: Edward Arnold).

CHAPLIN, Charles (1922) *My Trip Abroad* (New York and London: Harper & Brothers).

CHAPLIN, Charles (1964) *My Autobiography* (New York: Simon & Schuster).

CHAPLIN, Charles Jr., with N. and M. RAU (1960) *My Father, Charlie Chaplin* (London: Longmans).

CHAPLIN, Lita Grey, with Morton COOPER (1966) *My Life with Chaplin* (New York: Bernard Geiss).

CHARMLEY, John (1993) *Churchill: The End of Glory* (London: Hodder & Stoughton).

CHURCHILL, Randolph (1966) *Winston S. Churchill, Vol. 1: Youth 1874–1900* (London: Heinemann).

CHURCHILL, Sarah (1967) *A Thread in the Tapestry* (London: Andre Deutsch).

CLARK, Ronald W. (1988) *Lenin: The Man Behind the Mask* (London: Faber).

COBB, Richard (1972) *Reactions to the French Revolution* (Oxford University Press).

COHN, Norman (1972, orig. 1957) *The Pursuit of the Millennium* (London: Paladin).

COLEMAN, Ray (1984) *John Winston Lennon*, 2 vols. (London: Sidgwick & Jackson).

COLLIER, Peter and David HOROWITZ (1984) *The Kennedys* (London: Secker & Warburg).

CONGER, Jay A. and Rabindra N. KANUNGO, eds. (1988) *Charismatic Leadership: The Elusive Factor in Organizational Effectiveness* (San Francisco, London: Jossey-Bass).

DAVIES, Hunter (1979, orig, 1968) *The Beatles: The Authorized Biography* (London: Granada).

DAWIDOWICZ, Lucy (1983, orig, 1975) *The War against the Jews 1933–45* (Harmondsworth: Penguin Books).

DEUTSCHER, Isaac (1989, orig. 1949) *Stalin: a political biography* (Harmondsworth: Penguin Books).

ELIOT, T.S. (1953) *The Confidential Clerk* (London: Faber).

ELIOT, T.S. (1971) *The Waste Land: A facsimile and transcript of the original drafts* V. Eliot, ed. (London: Faber).

ELIOT, T.S. (1975, orig. 1933) *The Use of Poetry and the Use of Criticism* (London: Faber).

ELON, Amos (1972) *The Israelis: Founders and Sons* (New York: Bantam Books).

EFROS, Israel, ed. (1965, orig. 1948) *Poetic Works of H.N. Bialik* (New York: Bloch).

ERIKSON, Erik (1958) *Young Man Luther: a study in psychoanalysis and history* (New York: Norton).

ERIKSON, Erik (1969) *Gandhi's Truth* (New York: Norton).

ESPOSITO, John L. (1990) *Islam: The Straight Path* (New York: Oxford University Press).

FEST, Joachim (1974) *Hitler.* Tr. R. & C. Winston (New York: Harcourt Brace Jovanovich).

FICHMAN, Jacob (1946) *Bialik's Poetry* (Hebrew) (Jerusalem: Mossad Bialik).

FISCHER, Louis (1982, orig. 1951) *The Life of Mahatma Gandhi* (London: Granada).

FLOOD, Charles Bracelen (1989) *Hitler: The Path to Power* (London: Hamish Hamilton).

FREEMAN, Douglas (1948–57) *George Washington: A Biography*, 7 vols. (New York: Scribners).

FREUD, Sigmund (1933) *New Introductory Lectures on Psychoanalysis.* Vol. XXII in *The Standard Edition of the Complete Psychological Works of Sigmund Freud.* Tr. J. Strachey (London: Hogarth Press and The Institute of Psycho-Analysis).

FREUD, Sigmund, and Josef BREUER (1895) *Studies on Hysteria, Vol. II of The Standard Edition of the Complete Psychological Works of Sigmund Freud.* Tr. J. Strachey (London: Hogarth Press and The Institute of Psycho-Analysis).

FRIEDMAN, Maurice (1981) *Martin Buber's Life and Work: The Early Years – 1878–1923* Vol. 1 (New York: E.P. Dutton).

FRIEDRICH, Carl J. (1961) 'Political Leadership and the Problem of Charismatic Power.' *Journal of Politics* XXIII 1, 3–24.

FRIEDRICH, Carl J. (1972) *Tradition and Authority* (London: Macmillan).

FROMM, Erich (1977, orig. 1973) *The Anatomy of Human Destructiveness* (Harmondsworth: Penguin Books).

GABLER, Neal (1988) *An Empire of their Own: How the Jews Invented Hollywood* (New York: Anchor Books, Doubleday).

GALL, Lothar (1990, orig. 1980) *Bismarck: The White Revolutionary Vol. 1: 1815–1871.* Tr. J.A. Underwood (London: Unwin Hyman).

GILBERT, Martin (1971) *Winston S. Churchill, Vol. 3: The Challenge of War 1914–16* (London: Heinemann).

GILBERT, Martin (1983) *Winston S. Churchill, Vol. 6: Finest Hour 1939–41* (London: Heinemann).

GOLDMAN, Albert (1981) *Elvis* (Harmondsworth: Penguin Books).

GOLDMAN, Herbert G. (1988) *Jolson: The Legend Comes to Life* (New York, Oxford: Oxford University Press).

GREENBERG, Hayim (1968) 'A Day with Bialik.' In *Hayyim Greenberg Anthology*, M. Syrkin, ed. (Detroit: Wayne State University Press).

HAMILTON, Nigel (1992) *JFK: Reckless Youth* (London: Arrow).

HARRIS, Frank (1920) *Contemporary Portraits* (3rd series) (New York: published by the author).

HENGEL, Martin (1981, orig. 1968) *The Charismatic Leader and His Followers.* Tr. James C.G. Greig (Edinburgh: T. & T. Clark).

HIBBERT, Christopher (1962) *Benito Mussolini: A biography* (London: Longman).

HIBBERT, Christopher (1965) *Garibaldi and His Enemies* (London: Longman).

HIBBERT, Christopher (1980) *The French Revolution* (Harmondsworth: Penguin Books).

HYDE, H. Montgomery (1971) *Stalin: The History of a Dictator* (New York: Farrar, Straus & Giroux).

JAYAKAR, Popul (1986) *Krishnamurti: A Biography* (San Francisco: Harper & Row).

JORDAN, David P. (1985) *The Revolutionary Career of Maximilien Robespierre* (New York: The Free Press).

KERSHAW, Ian (1987) *The 'Hitler Myth:' Image and Reality in the Third Reich* (Oxford: Clarendon Press).

KERSHAW, Ian (1991) *Hitler* (London: Longman).

KLAUSNER, Joseph (1937) 'The First Public Lecture on Bialik and Its Consequences' (Hebrew) *Knesset* II 113–20.

KRISHNAMURTI, Jiddu (1976) *Krishnamurti's Notebook* (London: Gollancz).

LANGER, Walter (1972) *The Mind of Adolf Hitler* (New York: Basic Books).

LASSWELL, Harold D. (1960, orig. 1930) *Psychopathology and Politics* (New York: Viking Penguin),

LAWRENCE, D.H. (1960, orig. 1928) *Lady Chatterley's Lover* (Harmondsworth: Penguin Books).

LAWRENCE, T.E. (1973; orig. 1926) *The Seven Pillars of Wisdom* (London: Jonathan Cape).

LEMBOURN, H.J. (1979) *Forty Days with Marilyn* (London: Hutchinson).

LENNON, John (1980, orig. 1971) *Lennon Remembers: The Rolling Stone Interviews*, with Jan Wenner (London: Penguin Books).

LENNON, John (1981) Interview by D. Sheff with Lennon and Yoko Ono, *Playboy* 28, 1: 75–144.

LINCOLN, Abraham (1957) *Speeches and Letters 1832–1865*. Paul Angle, ed. (London: Dent; New York: E.P. Dutton).

LINDHOLM, Charles (1990) *Charisma* (Oxford: Blackwell).

LUTYENS, Mary (1975) *Krishnamurti: The Years of Awakening*, Vol. 1 (New York: Farrar, Straus and Giroux).

LUTYENS, Mary (1983) *Krishnamurti: The Years of Fulfilment*, Vol. 2 (London: John Murray).

LYONS, Timothy J. (1972) 'Roland H. Totteroh Interviewed.' *Film Culture*. Spring issue.

MANCHESTER, William (1983) *The Last Lion, Winston Spencer Churchill, Vol. I: Visions of Early: 1874–1932* (London: Michael Joseph).

MANCHESTER, William (1988) *The Last Lion, Winston Spencer Churchill, Vol. II: Alone 1932–1940* (New York: Laurel).

MARCUS, John T. (1961) 'Transcendence and Charisma.' *Western Political Quarterly*, XIV, 1: 236–41.

MATRAT, Jean (1975, orig. 1971) *Robespierre: Or the Tyranny of the Majority*. Tr. Alan Kendall (London: Angus & Robertson).

MAURIAC, François (1966) *De Gaulle*. Tr. Richard Howard (London: The Bodley Head).

McCABE, John (1978) *Charlie Chaplin* (London: Magnum, Methuen).

McINTOSH, William Currie, and William WEAVER (1983) *The Private Life of Cary Grant* (London: Sidgwick & Jackson).

MICHELS, Robert (1916) *Political Parties*. Tr. Eden & Cedar Paul (London: Jarrold & Sons).

MILLER, Arthur (1987) *Timebends: A Life* (London: Methuen).

MINNEY, R.J. (1954) *The Immortal Tramp* (London: Newnes Ltd).

MONROE, Marilyn (1974) *My Story*. Written by Ben Hecht (London: W.H. Allen).

MORAN, Lord (1966) *Winston Churchill: The Struggle for Survival 1940–1965* (London: Constable).

MORGAN, Ted (1985) *FDR: a biography* (New York: Simon & Schuster).

NETHERCOT, Arthur H. (1960) *The First Five Lives of Annie Besant* (London: Rupert Hart-Davis).

NEUMANN, Franz (1964) *The Democratic and the Authoritarian State: Essays in Political and Legal Theory* (Glencoe: Collier Macmillan).

ORLAN, Hayyim, ed. (1971) *Bialik's Poetry: an anthology* (Hebrew). (Tel Aviv: Dvir).

OSBORNE, Charles (1977) *Wagner and His World* (London: Thames & Hudson).

PAIS, Abraham (1982) *'Subtle is the Lord . . .': The Science and the Life of Albert Einstein* (Oxford University Press).

PARKES, Colin Murray (1986, orig. 1972) *Bereavement: Studies of Grief in Adult Life* (London: Tavistock Publications).

PONTING, Clive (1994) *Churchill* (London: Sinclair-Stevenson).

REEVES, Thomas C. (1991) *A Question of Character: A Life of John F. Kennedy* (London: Bloomsbury).

ROBERTS, J.M. (1978) *The French Revolution* (Oxford University Press).

ROBINSON, David (1983) *Chaplin: The Mirror of Opinion* (London: Secker & Warburg; Bloomington: Indiana University Press).

ROBINSON, David (1985) *Chaplin: His Life and Art* (London: Collins).

ROUSSEAU, Jean Jacques (1968, orig. 1762) *The Social Contract*. Tr. Maurice Cranston (Harmondsworth: Penguin Books).

RUDÉ, George (1975) *Robespierre: Portrait of a Revolutionary Democrat* (London: Collins).

RUDOLPH, Lloyd I. and Susanne Hoeber RUDOLPH (1983, orig. 1967) *Gandhi: The Traditional Roots of Charisma* (Chicago and London: University of Chicago Press).

SAMUEL, Maurice (1973, orig. 1943) *The World of Sholom Aleichem* (London: Valentine Mitchell).

SCHAMA, Simon (1989) *Citizens: A Chronicle of the French Revolution* (New York: Viking Penguin).

SCHIFFER, Irvine (1983) *Charisma: A Psychoanalytic Look at Mass Society* (Toronto: University of Toronto Press).

SCHLESINGER Jnr., Arthur (1960) 'On Heroic Leadership.' *Encounter*, XV 3–11.

SCHWARTZ, Barry (1987) *George Washington: The Making of an American Symbol* (New York: The Free Press).

SCHWEITZER, Arthur (1974) 'Theory of Political Charisma.' *Comparative Studies in Society and History*, XVI 2, 150–181.

SCHWEITZER, Arthur (1984) *The Age of Charisma* (Chicago: Nelson-Hall).

DE SELINCOURT, Ernest, and Helen, DARBISHIRE, eds. (1947) *The Poetical Works of William Wordsworth*, Vol. IV (Oxford University Press).

SENNETT, Richard (1986) *The Fall of Public Man* (London: Faber).

SHILS, Edward (1965) 'Charisma, Order, and Status.' *American Sociological Review* XXX 2, 199–213.

SMITH, Denis Mack (1956) *Garibaldi: A Great Life in Brief* (New York: Knopf).

SOBEL, Raoul, and David, FRANCIS (1977) *Chaplin: Genesis of a Clown* (London: Quartet).

SONNTAG, Jacob, ed. (1980) *Jewish Perspectives: 25 Years of Modern Jewish Writing* (London: Secker & Warburg).

STERN, J.P. (1975) *Hitler: The Führer and the People* (Glasgow: Fontana).

STEWART, Desmond (1974) *Herzl* (New York: Doubleday).

STORR, Anthony (1979) *The Art of Psychotherapy* (New York: Methuen).

SUENENS, Leon Joseph (1978) *Ecumenism and Charismatic Renewal: theological and pastoral orientations* (London: Darton, Longman & Todd).

SUMMERS, Anthony (1985) *Goddess: The Secret Lives of Marilyn Monroe* (London: Gollancz).

TALMON, Jacob (1986, orig. 1952) *The Origins of Totalitarian Democracy* (Harmondsworth: Penguin Books).

TALMON, Jacob (1967) *Romanticism and Revolt – Europe 1815–1848* (London: Thames & Hudson).

TAYLOR, A.J.P., ed. (1973) *Churchill: Four Faces and the Man* (Harmondsworth: Penguin Books).

TEVETH, Shabtai (1987) *Ben-Gurion: The Burning Ground 1886–1948* (Boston: Houghton Mifflin).

TOLAND, John (1977) *Adolf Hitler* (New York: Ballantine Books).

TRILLING, Lionel (1970) *The Liberal Imagination* (Harmondsworth: Penguin Books).

TUCKER, Robert C. (1968) 'The Theory of Charismatic Leadership.' *Daedalus* 97, 3: 731–56.

TULLY, Jim (1943) *A Dozen and One* (New York: Ambassador Books).

TUMARKIN, Nina (1983) *The Lenin Cult in Soviet Russia* (Cambridge, Mass. and London: Harvard University Press).

UNGERFELD, Moshe (1974) *Bialik and His Contemporaries* (Hebrew). (Tel Aviv: Am Hasefer).

WAITE, Robert (1977) *The Psychopathic God: Adolf Hitler* (New York: Basic Books).

WEATHERBY, W.J. (1977) *Conversations with Marilyn* (London: Sphere Books).

WEBER, Max (1968) *On Charisma and Institution Building*, S.N. Eisenstadt, ed. (Chicago and London: University of Chicago Press).

WHITE, Theodore H. (1962) *The Making of The President 1960* (London: Jonathan Cape).

WILLNER, Ann Ruth (1984) *The Spellbinders: Charismatic Political Leadership* (New Haven and London: Yale University Press).

WILSON, Bryan (1975) *The Noble Savages: The Primitive Origins of Charisma and its Contemporary Survival* (Berkeley: University of California Press).

WILSON, Jeremy (1989) *Lawrence of Arabia* (London: Heinemann).

WINNICOTT, Donald W. (1975) *The Maturational Processes and the Facilitating Environment* (London: Hogarth Press and The Institute of Psycho-Analysis).

WORDSWORTH, William (1975, orig. 1805, 1850) *The Prelude*, J.C. Maxwell, ed. (Harmondsworth: Penguin Educational).

ZAMOYSKI, Adam (1982) *Paderewski* (London: Collins).

Name Index

Subject Index

alien, charismatic as   10; alienation, overcoming of   10–11, 38, 107
amnesia   7, 8, 48, 56
amorality, propaganda for   xii, 106
anti-authoritarianism   56, 87, 87 n.
anti-Semitism   31–3, 37; *see also* pathology
appeal, charismatic   xi, xiii, 11, 14, 30, 31, 33, 41, 47, 50, 81, 83, 89, 90, 101, 106, 107; *see also* public, effect of charismatic on
art, charisma as   1, 88, 104, 106
aura, charismatic   46, 48, 79, 83

change   xiii, 108; charismatic does not   9, 19
charisma
  anti-bureaucratic   108
  cultivation of   107
  defined   ix, xii, 1, 7, 104
  distrust of   105
  immortality, agent of symbolic   107
  inoculation against trauma, as   107–8
  manipulation of   14, 26, 75
  moral neutrality of   xii, 108
  'rhetoric' of   26
  stabilizing effect of   25–7, 107
  stimulus   xii, 108
  swindle   107
  trivial use of   ix, 14, 75
  uncatchable   108
  warfare, triumph of one human life over dehumanizing   6
  weight on rickety building, as   107
  see also Weber *in Name Index*
childhood, broken or disrupted   *see* family disruption
childlessness   49, 66, 69–73, 76
correspondence, between internal and external reality   7, 9, 11, 24, 37, 38–9, 101, 104
  bereavement   72 (Ezekiel)

childhood and general social malaise   101 (Chaplin)
depression   21 (Churchill)   97 (Chaplin)
inferiority   77–8 (T.E. Lawrence)
infertility   72–3 (Bialik and T.S. Eliot)
freedom   14–15 (Kennedy)   77, 78 (T.E. Lawrence)
orphanhood   xiii, xiv, 65, 72, 73 (Bialik)
paralysis and hope   12 (Roosevelt)
psychosis   30–3 (Hitler)
union   9 (Bevin)   11 (Lincoln)
see also crisis, ideals and ideology
'cosmic consciousness'   x, xi, 83 (Marilyn Monroe)   x, 50ff. (Krishnamurti)   83 (Lennon); *see also* 'religion'
criminality   27ff., 90ff., 106; *see also* delinquency, genius
crisis   xii, ch. 1, 37, 104, 105, 106, 107; seeking of by charismatic   11; self-schooling in   xii, 10–11, 37; symbolic resolution through   11; *see also* correspondence, revolution, war

delinquency   81, 86, 90; *see also* criminality
depression   xii, 87, 106, 108; 12 (Roosevelt)   20–3, 24 (Churchill)   24, 28 (Hitler)   49 (Krishnamurti)   63, 64 (Bialik)   76 (T.E. Lawrence)   85 (Lennon)   96–7 (Chaplin); *see also* grief, pathology
Destiny   3–4, 20, 24, 43, 105
destruction   xiii, 5–6, 105, 108; *see also* crisis, violence, war

entertainment, charisma as   xii, 26, 80ff., 90, 105–6